Winning the Worry Battle

Life Lessons from the Book of Joshua

Barb Roose

D0062836

ABINGDON PRESS

NASHVILLE

WINNING THE WORRY BATTLE
LIFE LESSONS FROM THE BOOK OF JOSHUA

Library of Congress Cataloging-in-Publication Data has been requested.

ISBN 978-1-5018-5784-3

18 19 20 21 22 23 24 25 26—10 9 8 7 6 5 4 3 2 1
MANUFACTURED IN THE UNITED STATES OF AMERICA

Praise for *Winning the Worry Battle*

"I once heard that worry is the worship of our circumstances. As a young wife and mom, I knew I didn't want to worship my circumstances—I wanted to worship the One who could do something about my circumstances! Learning how to stop worry, however, was harder than I realized. I wish I'd had Barb's book back then. If worry, anxiety, and fear fill your thoughts, this book is for you, my friend."

—**Jill Savage**, author of *No More Perfect Moms* and *No More Perfect Marriages*

"Barb Roose gives us not only the reasons for the need to limit worry in our lives but also the practical and spiritual tools we need to do more than postpone worry and actually deal with it for the rest of our lives. I love her focus on the freedom that a life of worrying less can bring to each and every one of us. Highly recommended."

—**Kathi Lipp**, best-selling author of *The Husband Project, Clutter Free* and *Overwhelmed*

"Who doesn't want to win the worry battle? Whether it's our health, finances, or relationships, the mental hamster wheel of worry beckons us to constantly turn things over in our minds. Barb Roose shares valuable insights from the Book of Joshua and helps you apply them in very practical ways."

—**Melissa Spoelstra**, speaker and author of *Numbers* and *Total Family Makeover*

"This book is perfect for people like me who need tangible 1-2-3 advice on how to stop the worry cycle. Barb writes in a relatable fashion, sharing her personal struggles and making us feel connected. She's been there and isn't afraid to talk about it! It's a quick read and one anyone can appreciate!"

—**Kerri Pomarolli**, comedian with credits including *The Tonight Show* and Comedy Central, author of *Mom's Night Out and Other Things I Miss*

"Barb Roose brings Joshua, a man of tremendous faith in tumultuous times, to life. In her down-to-earth and tremendously encouraging way, she leads you to identify and release your worries in faith, strength, and freedom. Providing a treasure chest of tools and ideas that not only are beautiful but also keep you engaged and hungry for more of the Word of God, this book is for anyone longing to live a fuller, worry-free life of faith and freedom in the Lord!"

—**Melissa Maimone**, speaker and author of *Gathering Dandelions*

"Here's the truth: we all must battle against worry, doubt, and anxiety; some of us simply fight the battle more often. If you or someone you love is battling worry, read this book! There's no shame within these pages—only a mutual understanding of the real challenge of a life filled with fear. As you read, you will discover a hope rising within you that things are about to change for the better."

—**Susan Seay**, "Mentor 4 Moms" podcast host and author of *The Intentional Parent: Parenting on Purpose Even When Life Gets Busy*

"Whether worry creeps up on us from time to time or is an overwhelming presence in our lives, we all have room to grow! I'm so grateful for Barb's voice on this topic. Her bold determination coupled with sincere faith and compassion speak into the frenzy, empathizing and then encouraging and equipping us to fight against the worries we encounter. Take a deep breath, receive the coaching Barb offers, and step into the journey toward a life you crave, a life with less worry!"

—**Lauren Snyder**, Executive Director of Ministry, CedarCreek Church

"Friend, if you deal at all with worry, please, for your own sake and the sake of your family, read this book."

—**Shari Braendel**, founder of Fashion Meets Faith and author of *Help Me Jesus, I Have Nothing to Wear!*

To Dad…
Thank you for encouraging me to dream.

Contents

CONTENTS

Introduction

Do you ever make up horrible movies in your mind about getting in fatal car accidents or losing your kids at the zoo? I do. Are you the kind of person who hates not knowing how situations are going to turn out, and you drive yourself crazy figuring out possible solutions? Me too!

For years, I've struggled with automatically jumping to the worst-case scenario whenever uncertainty popped up in my life. In fact, I've spent many sleepless nights trying to figure out solutions to situations that were far out of my control.

As a Christian woman, I never understood why "just praying about it" didn't ease my worry battle. Many times, I've thought that there was something wrong with my faith or that God was mad at me because I worried too much.

About fifteen years ago, I encountered a season of life when worry wore me out! I was a mess and knew that I couldn't keep living that way. Out of desperation, I dove deep into Bible study and learned how to fight in faith, instead of freaking out in fear.

If worry is wearing you out, then God's got a new way forward for you! Join me for a journey filled with lots of stories that you can relate to as well as powerful life lessons from a man in the Bible who fought a worry battle too. His name was Joshua. As we experience his story, you'll learn how to battle worry with many new tools that you can use for the rest of your life.

INTRODUCTION

While I was writing this book, my wonderful father, Bobby, was diagnosed with metastatic lung cancer. I used the tools in this book to fight fear and worry so that I wouldn't lose a precious moment of time with my dad, who passed away just eight days after his diagnosis.

Just as God gave Joshua and the Israelites victory over uncertainty and worry, He wants to do the same for you. We're going to find real encouragement to overcome our daily struggles and the bigger battles we all face. When you learn how to battle worry and experience victory, your life will be blessed and you'll be transformed in radical ways.

Are you ready? Let's do this!

What Kind of Worrier Are You?

That is why I tell you not to worry about everyday life.

—Matthew 6:25

hy did I let my mind go there AGAIN?
There I stood, in my kitchen, swiping at the tears rolling down my face. Was I crying about something that had just happened? No. I was sobbing over a horrible mental movie generated in my mind about one of my girls getting into a fatal car accident as she drove to her friend's house.

That movie was so graphic, so real, that I could have won Academy Awards for best actress, best screenplay, and best special effects. I could see the accident scene and myself running and screaming toward a mangled car with hazy smoke rising from the wreck. I could see the EMTs pulling me away from cradling my child as they said, "Ma'am, she's gone. Let her go, ma'am." I could hear my screams in my mind. My heart pounded and tears streamed down my face. *Why does this feel so real, even though it's only in my mind?*

Then I'd snap back to reality. I was worn out. I felt guilty and foolish. Guilty because I'd imagined something that really has happened to others but not to me. Foolish because I should know better. *C'mon, Barb! You've made yourself upset over something that wasn't even real.*

By definition, the word *worry* means "to torment one's self with or suffer from disturbing thoughts."[1] Have you ever found yourself watching a mental movie about an imaginary tragic event in your life, yet you couldn't stop watching even though it made you cry real tears? Almost every single one of us has spent time worrying about the bad things that could happen—whether they involve our families, our jobs, our finances, our health, or our futures.

Lately, it feels as though our world has gone a little cuckoo. A few minutes on social media brings on heart flutters for some and an outright freak-out for others. Have you ever spent a sleepless night worrying about the state of our nation or world? You aren't alone. If I had a dime for every time I've worried about something in my life, I might be tempted to start worrying about where to store all those dimes!

Take a moment to engage in a quick "temperature check" on your current level of worry. On a scale of 1 to 5, how much worry are you experiencing in your life right now?

1. No worries
2. Just a few
3. More than a few
4. Mind is racing
5. Overwhelmed with a lot of worries

For much of my teen years, through my thirties, I hovered between a 4 and a 5. I felt like a bad Christian because I struggled so hard with worry. Why did "just pray about it" not work for me? I *did* pray about it, but I still worried! While there were some women who said that they were "too blessed to be stressed," I was a five-foot-ten ball of stress all the time! Why couldn't I just give my worries to God and let them go? Was there something wrong with my faith?

Perhaps that kind of uncomfortable honesty is difficult for you to hear. But I want to believe that a few of you have let out a relieved sigh instead. You aren't alone in the battle against worry. You've tried to push back against it, and yet it keeps pulling you in anyway. That push-pull, back-and-forth battle is exhausting, as you first try to resist worry and then realize how it feels after worry has whipped you around a bit. I get it. I've lived it. Yet God has shown me how to wake up each day and claim victory over any worry that comes my way. I'd love to tell you more about how you can claim God's victory too.

Do you know how much time you spend worrying? One study quantified that even people not diagnosed with a specific anxiety disorder spent 55 minutes every day worrying about something.[2] Since there are 1,440 minutes per day, that might not seem like much. However, the time you spend fretting, freaking, or flipping out really adds up. Let's look at how many minutes you might have already spent worrying in your life if you're "normal."

If you are 20 years old, you've spent up to 401,500 minutes worrying.
If you are 30 years old, you've spent up to 602,250 minutes worrying.
If you are 40 years old, you've spent up to 803,000 minutes worrying.
If you are 50 years old, you've spent up to 1,003,750 minutes worrying.
If you are 60 years old, you've spent up to 1,204,500 minutes worrying.
If you are 70 years old, you've spent up to 1,405,250 minutes worrying.

Here's where I'm going to geek out on you a little more: Did you know that forty million adults in the United States are affected by an anxiety disorder?[3] If you're struggling with anxiety or worry, whether it's been diagnosed or not, you are not alone!

This means that one in five adults deals with an anxiety disorder that interferes with their daily lives. Imagine that one of those adults lives in your house. Maybe you grew up in a home with one parent who struggled with worry and anxiety or had a grandparent, aunt, or uncle struggling with worry. Here are some examples that might sound familiar:

You miss curfew by fifteen minutes, and when you come home, your mom screams and yells at you for an hour because she just *knew* that you were dead in a ditch because you didn't call.

Your dad flips out if you leave the lights on or ruin a piece of clothing because he worries all of the time about money.

Your grandmother leaves messages on your cell phone each day to make sure you didn't get kidnapped on your way home from your part-time job at the mall.

Perhaps *you* are the one in five. How many times have you said, "I'm so sorry for flipping out on you guys" because you freaked out about something? If you want to be a better influence around your friends, spouse, or kids, then fighting your worry battle may be the best gift you can give the people around you. Ask yourself: *Do I want my kids to grow up and handle worry like I'm handling it now?* Or *What can I learn so that I can teach the people around me how to handle worry in a healthy, God-honoring way?*

Mental health professionals tell us that worrying is normal. And since research seems to indicate that everyone worries, we need to be aware and seek treatment if our normal worry becomes excessive. Unlike taking your temperature to find out if you have a fever, there isn't an objective test for worry, but there are inventories, like the Penn State Worry Questionnaire, to help you determine how much worry is interfering with your life.[4] Maybe you've been to the doctor or another mental health professional and he or she used words such as *generalized anxiety disorder, social anxiety disorder, panic disorder,* and *obsessive compulsive disorder* to diagnose your worry or anxiety based on its intensity and influence on your life. If not, it would be wise for you to talk with your doctor or mental health professional if worry interferes with your home or work life.

You may have to battle worry each day, but worry doesn't have to wreck your life. In this book, we'll focus on battling worry, no matter how severely it impacts your life. God's power and promises to give you victory over your worry battle aren't limited by how severe your battle may be. You may have to fight a little harder, but God's victory will be that much bigger for you!

What Kind of Worrier Are You?

I like to picture life as being like a seven-layer Mexican salad. I'm smiling as I write these words because I really love that dish. If you don't, picture your life as any other kind of multilayered dish. (If you're part of my generation, you may even remember the classic episode of *Friends* in which Rachel accidentally combined two recipes and made an unforgettable trifle with layers of ladyfingers, jam, custard, raspberries, and beef with peas and onions in a large glass bowl. Ross's response to her creation: "It tastes like feet."[5])

Each layer of a seven-layer dish represents the foundation and progress of my life, and consequently, those layers are deeply woven into my worry battle. The bottom layers represent the influence of my parents and other relatives, my education, my self-image, my life experiences, and my spiritual journey. The top layers are more recent experiences and my current environment. Research tells us that our environment can influence what we worry about.[6]

If you've seen a seven-layer dish at the end of a party or family gathering, you know that the layers are often mixed together—and sometimes quite messy. The same happens with our lives. Over time, I've become the sum of everything that I've seen, heard, and experienced. One of my favorite anonymous quotes is, "What forms you, follows you."

Based on what I've experienced and observed both in my life and over a dozen years of working in ministry leadership and as a professional life coach, I've recognized the following identities, each categorized according to how they react to worry. Even if you don't like being pigeonholed into one category or another, it might be helpful to understand the different ways that women can manifest worry. Perhaps you will even discover that the difficult-to-deal-with behaviors of your mother, sister, grandmother, or friend may not be because she wants to hassle you, but because she's dealing with her own worry battle.

	Passive	Active
Few words	Silent Sufferer	Busy Body
	Keeps all of her fears and worries to herself	*Overworks to control worry*
Lots of words	Mother Hen	Control Freak
	Nags others to feel calmer	*Manipulates to reduce fear and worry*

The *silent sufferer* struggles in silence, and her friends have no idea how bad she's really struggling. Sadly, she can't stop rehearsing tragedy. In severe cases, our silent sufferer is actually in physical pain because of her anxiety.

The *busy body*—not to be confused with the annoying *busybody*, whom nobody wants around—is the friend that we love to have around because she organizes, calls, picks up, drops off, and cleans out. Incomplete tasks are worry triggers for her, so this is why she also tends to overplan and is often overwhelmed.

Mother hens cluck, cluck, cluck, which is a creative way of saying that they nag, nag, nag all the time. A mother hen will call you ten times a day to check on you. Mother hens believe that their reminders and long lectures are helpful and keep people safe. They can be blind to the fact that friends or family have stopped listening to them. Even though the mother hen means well, her love and concern feel suffocating.

Control freaks use words such as *helpful, diligent, detail-oriented,* or *type A.* They convince themselves that their perspective is what's best for the highest good. That's why control freaks justify attempts to steer friends and loved ones' choices or manipulate the consequences.

Did you find yourself in any of those descriptions? Maybe you fit into more than one of the responses to worry. I did feel a little conflicted about introducing these different categories because I don't want you to get stuck on a label. A negative label has the potential to reinforce negative mind-sets and behaviors. But if we can tell ourselves the truth and treat ourselves with compassion (instead of beating ourselves up), then we're ready to take a positive next step to the future.

Taking a First Step in the Right Direction

Change is scary, but let's be honest: living worn out by worry isn't exactly a party either. The first step in the right direction is *willingness*, which is based on your own power to choose. Ask yourself these three questions to decide if you are willing to win the battle against worry:

1. Are you tired of living a worn-out, freaked-out, flipped-out-by-worry life?
2. Are you ready to give up your old habits to fight worry God's way, even if you have to learn new tools and behaviors?
3. Will you allow God to change your heart, mind, or even your life in order to give you victory?

As part of learning how to battle worry in a new way, you're going to learn some important life lessons from the Old Testament Book of Joshua—and you don't have to be a Bible scholar to absorb them. You'll find inspiration and encouragement as God teaches Joshua how to fight his worry battle. Even if you think you're familiar with Joshua's story, trust me: there is always more that we can learn about trusting God's promises, being courageous in uncertain times, and developing the strength to hold on and hang on no matter what life throws our way.

What's more, the life lessons you learn will also include many powerful, practical tools that you can use every day in your worry battle. You can begin to use these tools no matter where you are spiritually. You're going to battle worry every day of your life, but with these tools, you can position yourself to win over worry every single day! I've been a Christian for a long time, and I believe that these tools become more effective the more I continue to use them!

If you need a getting-started tool to help you with worry today, grab a little stone and call it your "worry stone." A worry stone is carried in your pocket, and rubbing the stone between your thumb and index finger can have a calming effect. In addition to calming the physical stress, we want to calm our minds with God's truth. So, as you rub the stone, repeat the following: "I don't have to worry; God will help me." (If you don't like the idea of a stone in your pocket, you can also use a four-by-four-inch square of soft fabric.)

Dream of Victory!

Complete victory is when we know that God is with us and for us in every situation, whether real or imagined. We're on the path to victory when we lean into God's presence during real crisis or tragedy. We're also on the path to victory when our thoughts focus on God's power and presence as we ponder the future, instead of imagining problems that haven't happened yet.

Can you dream of victory over worry in your life? Here are some things that I want you to begin dreaming about. Circle or make note of three that you want to experience most:

Finally finding peace.	Learning to stay calm.	Modeling peace/calm for others.
Not running away.	Moving forward even in fear.	Making a big, bold decision.
Getting up after failure.	Holding steady in tough times.	Taking on a new adventure.

When I began my worry battle over fifteen years ago, God had to teach me to stay calm, and I wanted to teach my children how to stay calm. I didn't want them to grow up thinking, *Oh, there goes Mom, flipping out again.* As God taught me how to use the tools that you'll learn in this book, I learned how to shut down those horrible mental movies whenever worry began to creep into my life. I've learned how to build courage through training spiritually for tough times, and I've become strong in my faith by saying yes to God in obedience. Now, I no longer spend my days fighting fear because God has taught me how to fight in faith. You can do this too!

If victory could be summed up in a feeling, it would be peace. It's that *ahhhh* feeling you get when everything around you is crazy, but you feel calm and can make calm decisions. In John 14:27, Jesus tells us of a precious gift. He says, "I am leaving you with a gift—peace of mind and heart. And the peace I give is a gift the world cannot give. So don't be troubled or afraid."

The world tells us that we can buy peace of mind, but we can't. Peace is truly a gift! And Philippians 4:7 tells us that the peace that God gives is beyond the world's understanding. No matter how hard we try, we can't manufacture lasting peace on our own. Peace is God's secret sauce for victorious living.

My dream is that you will chase God's path toward victory so that you'll be blessed every day by God's peace. I want you to wake up each day and reach toward God's abundance for your life instead of waking up in fear and worry.

⁓

Here's one final thought:
Today is the last day of my life that I need to be hopelessly stuck in fear and worry.

2

Cliffhangers

It is impossible to remove cliffhangers from your life, but God's hope is your strong ledge to stand on.

—Barb Roose

I felt as if I had a raging case of PMS.

In spring 1999, I won my company's top sales award and an all-expense-paid trip to Zimbabwe with my husband. Our trip was scheduled for the following June. Even as I smiled in response to others' congratulations and excitement about our upcoming trip, behind my smile was a struggle that I could barely contain. What should have been one of the best seasons of my life was wrapped in tears, stress, and anxiety.

Prior to this opportunity, I'd only traveled around the United States, and not abroad. In my mind, Africa was a paper map that I'd memorized for my junior high geography class, filled with dozens of strange names and amoeba-like boundaries.

When I realized that we'd won an opportunity to travel to the massive continent, my mind tripped over what could best be described as *uncertainty,* or the situations in our lives where the ending has a question mark.

Uncertainty can have one of the following endings: a good ending, a bad ending, a mixed ending, or a surprise ending. But there's also one more kind of ending, my most hated form of uncertainty: the ending that never seems to come.

When I think about uncertainty, the word *cliffhanger* comes to mind. Before streaming media, American television audiences watched regular episodes of our favorite shows from September through May. Back then, we would rearrange our schedules to make sure we were in front of our televisions for the final regular episode of the season. Once those shows ended, we had to wait until the new season began the next fall to watch the outcome to the precarious or hilarious situation we had been left with. *Who shot JR? Would Ross marry Rachel? Is the hatch light on? Who survived the Greys' plane crash?* Even though we hated heading back to school in August, we couldn't wait to see what was happening with our favorite shows in September. The night of the *Friends* season premiere, with Ross and Emily at the altar, I locked the door of my room and took my phone off the hook. (You see, in ancient times, our telephones were mounted on walls. If you took the handset off the main part of the phone, then no one could reach you. It's the modern equivalent of blocking everyone all at once.)

Now we have streaming media, and while cliffhangers exist, the timelines have changed. Shows like *Doctor Who, Sherlock,* and *Call the Midwife* air their season finales, and then fans wait up to two years in some cases to see what happened to their heroes or their favorite characters. *Is Moriarty back? Will Sheldon and Amy get married?*

While we embrace the *will they or won't they?* in our television shows and movies, we generally reject uncertainty in our lives. If I'm driving to a new area without a map to tell me where to go, that uncertainty immediately produces stress. If you've gone on a first date with a guy and he doesn't make the promised call,

> Uncertainty is at the heart of our insecurity.

that uncertainty produces stress. When you feel an unknown lump, that cliffhanger creates stress.

When I'm not sure which way a situation will go in my life, it's hard not to imagine myself hanging by my fingertips on a ledge that's a thousand feet high over a canyon. That would be a little less stressful, right? In that moment of uncertainty, the biggest question on my mind is *WWHMe?* Do you remember *WWJD,* or *What Would Jesus Do?* Well, WWHMe captures the core of my struggle in the cliffhanger moment: *What Will Happen to Me?*

Uncertainty is at the heart of our insecurity. It's hard to move about difficult circumstances if we're not sure whether or not we'll be okay. It's hard to make good decisions when we're not sure if we need to protect ourselves from potential physical, emotional, financial, or spiritual harm. So, what do we do? We use tactics like nagging, manipulation, and control to try to remove the question marks from our lives. But even though we put on our Sherlock detective hats to find out the how, what, or why to whatever we can't figure out, that doesn't actually mean that we'll eliminate uncertainty.

How many times have you gotten even more frustrated because you moved heaven and earth to find answers, but all of your effort created more questions?

I found a breast lump on the evening of my thirty-eighth birthday. I kept asking myself, *Is this what I think it is?* I thought I'd be okay if I could get a mammogram as soon as possible. After the mammogram, there was more uncertainty, so the doctor ordered a biopsy. After the biopsy, I faced an entirely new crop of uncertainties that kept me spinning round and round. Eventually, the biopsy results were negative, but enduring that period of uncertainty positively turned my life upside down.

There's actually a theory called the Heisenberg uncertainty principle,[1] which states that it is impossible to know simultaneously the exact position and momentum of any given particle. This principle, if applied to everyday life, would mean that you can't know everything at all times. This concept, like kryptonite, cripples control freaks like me. What are the cliffhangers in your life these days? Is there a place in your life where you feel you are hanging off the edge with no safety net underneath? Or maybe your cliffhanger looks like a closed door that you can't see behind, or two doors with only one good outcome. Does your cliffhanger look more like a sadistic game of Russian roulette and you're wondering if you or a loved one will be saved or will suffer? Other cliffhangers look like the text bubble on an iPhone while you're waiting for someone to finish a message. Doesn't it drive you crazy when someone starts a message and you see those three dots, but ten minutes later you can't put your phone down because you're still waiting for his or her reply?!

All of our life cliffhangers revolve around one or more of the seven *f*s of life: family, friends, firm (work), finances, faith, fun (recreation), or fitness (health).[2]

As you reflect on those unresolved situations in your life, how much stress does that uncertainty rev up in your heart? We like our lives to be like our Christmas gifts, neatly tied with a bow on top. Comedienne Gilda Radner captured that sentiment when she wrote, "I wanted a perfect ending.... Now I've learned, the hard way, that some poems don't rhyme, and some stories don't have a clear beginning, middle, and end.... Life... is about not knowing, having to change, taking the moment and making the best of it, without knowing what's going to happen next."[3]

One study showed forty-five individuals two rocks and asked participants to predict which rock might have a snake hiding underneath.[4] (Some of you are stressed now and you aren't even in the study!) The study tested the amount of stress people experienced while trying to decide if there was or wasn't a snake underneath. Here's what's interesting: those who knew there was a snake under the rock felt less stress than those who were uncertain.

In our favorite television series, a cliffhanger was dangled in front of us, which brought us back to the same series in the fall. In real-life cliffhangers, the stress of uncertainty can actually send us over the edge mentally, physically, emotionally, and relationally.

As I prepared for my trip to Africa, I often felt overwhelmed by the stress of uncertainty. While my company sent step-by-step instructions on how to prepare for the trip of a lifetime and gave us a comprehensive view of our itinerary, I still stressed out over WWHMe. In fact, I talked my husband out of a trip extension to Botswana because I could barely handle the uncertainty of visiting Zimbabwe. It didn't matter that I saw photos of our hotel or the beautiful Victoria Falls; I still didn't know what my experience would be, and that stressed me. *What will it be like to fly for twenty-two hours straight? Will I be able to get my kids everything they need while we're gone? What will the food look like? What will the bathrooms look like? How close are the lions to us? Are there spiders? Will I ruin this trip because I'm so stressed?*

When I look back on the months leading up to the trip, I wish I could go back to my younger self and share the wisdom that I've learned over the years. Then again, it was her journey that began the path to where I find myself today. So, if I could go back to see her again, I'd just give her a hug and ask how I could help.

If you're overwhelmed by the stress of uncertainty, you are among friends. We're all facing one or more cliffhangers in our lives. Some of our cliffhangers are like final season episodes that will be resolved in a few months and life will go on again until new cliffhangers show up. But if you're like me, there's one or two cliffhangers that have been hanging on for a few years now. One of the scariest cliffhangers in my life has had me dangling by my fingertips on the edge for a few years. I wish I knew how or when it might end, but I don't.

While our lives may feel like we're dangling on the edge, there's an invisible, yet hope-sustaining ledge that we can rest our feet upon in uncertainty.

At the Edge of Uncertainty

After forty years of wandering the desert in the same clothes, eating the same food, and watching their parents and grandparents die along the way, a group of weary people arrived on the edge of the great unknown. Over a million Israelites gathered east of the Jordan River. On the other side of the river was their new homeland, Canaan.

As much as I'd like to talk about the miracle of clothes that didn't wear out for four decades (Deuteronomy 8:4), what's even more shocking is that the millions gathered by the lush Jordan should have arrived at that destination after only eleven days, not forty years (Deuteronomy 1:2).

If you aren't familiar with what happened, the record of the Israelites' self-inflicted misadventure is documented in the Old Testament texts. The general summary of the situation boils down to bad attitudes, multiple rebellions, and a whole lot of fear over uncertainty.

Now, after four hundred years of slavery in Egypt and an additional forty years wandering around the Sinai Peninsula, a land bridge that connects Africa and Asia still today, the Israelites had finally arrived at the edge of their new homeland.

But what would happen next? Moses, the leader of the Israelites, gave a long message filled with everything the Israelites would need to know before they entered. God had given Moses the entire playbook, cookbook, standard operating procedures, and penal code as well as a praise and worship songbook for the people to learn, know, and live.

Imagine that you're an Israelite mother listening to Moses address the assembly. Okay, you're *trying* to listen, but you're shushing your kids every two minutes so that you can hear. While your parents and grandparents died during the desert years, you've talked with your adult siblings at night about what it will be like to finally reach your new home. You've heard a few descriptions of what this new land is like, but the reports were conflicted. Before they died, your parents told you about some men who'd scouted the new land just after leaving Egypt. Those men had described the land as "flowing with milk and honey" (Exodus 3:8). Your parents told you about a single cluster of grapes so large that two scouts had to carry it on a pole between them. But they also warned you that fighting to conquer the land would be dangerous because there were powerful people living in well-protected cities, and there were even giants.

So, as you stand and listen to Moses while your children play tag around your tunic, you wonder: *Will I be happy? Will we be safe? What will our lives be like on the other side of that great river Jordan? Where will I get water each day to do the laundry or cook dinner? How long will my brothers and husband be away at battle?*

As those cliffhanger questions lingered in one young mother's mind that day, there was a hope that at least a few cliffhangers were finally put to rest. No more kids asking, "Are we there yet?" No more packing and unpacking tents. Most of all, she can shake the years of sand out of her stuff!

We're going to check in with our Israelite friend throughout the book to see how she and the other Israelites managed their journey into the Promised Land and navigated uncertainty and other issues, like fear and worry. While the Israelites may have lived thousands of years ago, the stress of uncertainty and worry hasn't changed. Perhaps as you read about their worry battle, you will find a new path forward toward victory over yours.

Find Your Ledge in Uncertainty

God has no cliffhangers.

So, why does God allow those cliffhanger moments in our lives? Isn't God aware of how hard uncertainty is on us?

God, can you just tell me if my mom will survive her cancer?

God, when will we get on the other side of this financial hardship?

God, will I ever meet the person who will love me until death parts us?

God, will I ever accept having this disease?

God, is there any hope for my child's addiction?

When one of my daughters was diagnosed with Asperger's syndrome in middle school, my already-breaking heart completely crumbled. I went to the gym each day and cried out to God while running on the treadmill. Asperger's makes it difficult for people to create meaningful connections with others. I knew I wouldn't always

> We can only see our situation from our perspective. Our challenge is to look at uncertainty from God's point of view.

be around, and the thought of my brilliant, gifted, sweet girl without someone to share her life with undid all of this mother's heart. As I ran, my heart cried out to God, *Will she ever be able to fall in love, God?*

Years earlier, our family had endured a very stressful financial season. An unexpected tax bill, combined with loss of employment and several health crises, made us feel we were falling down a black hole that seemed to have no bottom. During those years, I kept asking God, *When will this end? Will it ever end?* At other times, I got really angry with God because I felt like I was dangling off the cliff of uncertainty and my fingers were losing their grip.

Depending on how you were raised, you might feel guilty about being angry with God. If you believe that God is capable of anything, you might be angry that He hasn't answered your prayer for the cliffhanger to come to an end. I've been a Christian since I was nine years old, and yet, I have journals with the phrase, "When will it end, God?" repeated over and over again. If this sounds like you, it's okay to feel angry in your uncertainty. It's okay if you're angry with God. Your next best move is to tell Him about it, as a man named David did long ago:

> How long, O Lord, will you look on and do nothing?
> Rescue me from [my enemies'] fierce attacks.
> Protect my life from these lions!
> Then I will thank you in front of the great assembly.
> I will praise you before all the people.
> —Psalm 35:17-18

Do you feel like God sees your cliffhanger but He's in heaven, munching on chips and watching your life like a Netflix episode while you twist in the wind? Don't feel guilty if you've ever whispered, "If God cared, He'd hurry up and help."

There's an organic flaw embedded in our WWHMe mentality: we can only see our situation from our perspective. Our challenge is to look at uncertainty from God's point of view. Here's the truth: our uncertainty isn't a problem for God.

God is totally comfortable leaving open-ended timelines, resolutions, or direction of our lives. What feels like a cliffhanger to us isn't to God. But how do we learn how to see uncertainty from God's perspective so, rather than feeling like we're slipping, we stand firm? Imagine looking at every new situation in your life and knowing without a doubt that you will be okay, even if the worst happens.

> God protects me with what He doesn't give me as much as He blesses me with what He does give me.

It is impossible to remove cliffhangers from your life, but God's hope is your strong ledge to stand on. We can't know everything about every area of our lives at all times. This means that you may need to acknowledge that voice of pride that whispers, *But you can figure this out.* This voice is the same one that answered Eve in the garden of Eden when she said that the fruit was forbidden: "'You won't die!' the serpent replied to the woman. 'God knows that your eyes will be opened as soon as you eat it, and you will be like God, knowing both good and evil'" (Genesis 3:4-5).

In my struggle to deal with uncertainty, I've had two eye-opening moments:

1. I can't know everything that God knows.
2. I don't want to be responsible for knowing everything that God knows.

We think that knowing everything will relieve the stress of uncertainty in our lives. That's the lie that pride whispers to us in the pain of uncertainty. While we would like to know everything that will happen to us, that is a burden of knowledge that we cannot bear.

Instead, God wisely decided that He would hold onto knowledge and only give us responsibility for the knowledge He gives to us. In his long message to the Israelites before they entered the Promised Land, Moses said to them: "The Lord our God has secrets known to no one. We are not accountable for them, but we and our children are accountable forever for all that he has revealed to us, so that we may obey all the terms of these instructions" (Deuteronomy 29:29).

As theologian Wayne Grudem says, "This God who is omniscient (all-knowing) has absolutely certain knowledge; there can never be any fact that he does not already know; thus, there can never be any fact that would prove that something God thinks is actually false."[5]

If you trust that God knows all things, then is it possible for you to trust that in your moment of uncertainty, He has only given you the set of circumstances that you can handle at this time? As time goes on, God will give you more, whether it's information or capacity. I've learned that often, God protects me with what He doesn't give me as much as He blesses me with what He does give me.

That's a lot to absorb if you're dangling on the cliff of scary uncertainty. Even if you can't believe what I've just proposed 100 percent, is it possible for you to do one thing? Can you start with believing that statement just a little? Can you begin to believe that God has given you only the knowledge and resources you can handle right now? Whatever you are missing in your life is where God is planning to either provide or increase your knowledge and capacity. Either way, God's got a plan to keep you safe and secure in your uncertainty.

Would you like a tool to help you calm down during uncertainty and chaos? I want to teach you the CALM Technique. I use this technique to settle down my out-of-control emotions and to regain my focus on God. Here's how you do it:

> Step 1: **C**ount to five by inhaling on the number and exhaling the word *Mississippi*.
> Step 2: **A**cknowledge God's presence by saying "God, I know that you are here with me right now."
> Step 3: **L**ist where you need God's help.
> Step 4: **M**editate and repeat the following: "God is here, and He will take care of me/this."

Here's the takeaway from what we're talking about:
I am safe when I believe God knows what is best for me and those I love.

3

Eight-Legged Worry

Worry often is a small thing that casts a big shadow.

—Swedish Proverb

On what should have been a glorious morning, I faced two choices: I could suffocate to death, or become a supersize, tasty snack for the hairy eight-legged monster lurking somewhere in my room.

I pondered my options while stuffed inside a comforter wrapped tighter than a burrito around me. My panting breaths heated the inside of that comforter—hotter than the green hot sauce that my husband fancies when he doctors up his *barbacoa*. I needed to breathe, but did I want to risk dying? Loosening the comforter increased the odds that a ginormous arachnid might creep inside. And that would just not do.

Unwilling to risk such a horrible situation, I clutched the comforter tighter around my sweltering skin. There was a better chance that I'd win the Powerball than that spider would get inside with me. My fitful dreams cycled between Facebook notifications of my spider-induced death and the faces of beloved girlfriends who'd make sure that the eyebrows on my corpse looked on point one final time.

Here's the kicker: I woke up the next morning and I wasn't bitten—mainly because there was never a spider!

I had spent eight hours fearing this creature, as well as a litany of outcomes that never happened. I'd lost sleep and suffocated myself all because I'd been trapped by an *eight-legged worry.*

> The fear of our fear is actually our worry.

At the center of eight-legged worry is something or someone we fear, like snakes, spiders, airplanes, chewing gum, or dying. That fear is like the body of a spider. Some of our fears are small, like a tiny daddy longlegs; others are huge, like a tarantula's body. One of the original meanings of the word *fear* comes from an old Saxon word that meant "to terrify."

The fear of our fear is actually our worry. As our fear persists without relief, we begin to ask "what if" questions, as if preparing for the eventuality that we're going to have to confront our fears or maneuver to prevent them from coming true. I saw an Internet ad for a one-handed collapsible stroller. An expectant couple was reviewing the stroller when the husband asked, "Do we really need a one-handed collapsible stroller?" His pregnant wife's eyes widened. She replied, "Well, if we don't get it, then we'll have to put the baby down while we collapse the stroller. What if she gets into the front seat and drives off?" The husband replied, "We're getting the stroller."

Those "what if" questions are like the spider legs that extend from the body of our fear, hence eight-legged worry. Like a spider's legs, our worries tumble over each other but skitter out of control until we're overwhelmed. Here's one woman's story:

> I had my first anxiety attack when I was eight years old. I thought it was a heart attack. I went to the free clinic in our neighborhood and asked if someone could help me. They gave me a EKG, took my blood pressure, and asked me what was

going on and why I came by myself. I told them I was alone. My mom was at work and my brothers were with friends. I was worried we were not going make rent that month. There wasn't enough food in the house. I couldn't eat all the time so that my brothers and mom would have enough.

I was worried that I couldn't protect us if someone broke into our house. I was walking around trying to "figure it all out."

All of a sudden I wasn't able to breathe right and my heart beat too hard and fast; nothing seemed real. I sat down on the curb and cried until I could breathe again. That's when I went to the free clinic.

But after the EKG, they told me I was overreacting to something and my body reacted to it. They said that I was fine; nothing was wrong with me. I believed this to be true until I was twenty-six and a doctor told me that these episodes were called anxiety/panic attacks. I suffered from these all my life and never told anyone until I was twenty-six, when I almost drove my car into a telephone pole because it didn't seem real.

Today I have counseling and medication, but the worry never goes away.

Does this story resonate with you? Perhaps you have a different story or you didn't begin to worry until later in life. We don't need to compare our stories. Worry is worry, no matter the circumstances. Don't diminish your worry problem by thinking that it's nothing compared to someone else's.

What are you afraid of right now? You might be struggling to narrow down the list, but pick just one fear for now. (Don't worry; eventually we're going to tackle all of your fears. You'll not only be able to pluck all the legs off your worry but also learn how to crush that juicy middle too.)

Take a piece of paper and write down that fear at the center of the page, like the body of a spider. Then list all of the what-if scenarios that extend from your fear like the legs from a spider. How do you feel after listing all of those worries?

When I think about my eight-legged worry, my body worries too. Whereas fear hastens my heartbeat and causes my eyes to dart back and forth, worry produces more of a low-bass buzz in my body that isn't apparent to anyone else but that I can't ignore. Sometimes, worry churns up sickening nausea that bubbles like an unerupted volcano and makes me want to vomit. At other times, worry lays a rotten egg in the pit in my stomach that ruins my appetite. When it is time to go to bed, worry keeps me awake as the "what if" worst-case endings scurry back and forth across my mind like the baby spiders from the burst egg sac at the end of *Charlotte's Web*. (As a child, I braved the book until Charlotte became a mama. As soon as her egg sac hatched, I dropped that book like it was hot. There's an unfinished book report out there somewhere because I'm not completely sure how the story ended.)

When I asked a group of people what their lives could be like if they eliminated worry, it's no surprise that they longed to experience a greater quality of life. After my sleepless night wrapped like a burrito, I was exhausted the next day. While I may have suffered from lack of sleep, the real culprit was worry.

It's one thing for our eight-legged worry to feel like a harmless daddy longlegs, but what if you've got crowd-clearing, tarantula-size worry terrorizing your heart and mind and you can't kill it?

> My fourteen-year-old daughter started hanging out with the "drug crowd." They made her feel welcomed. It was four years of fighting and sleepless nights. Fear and worry

started manifesting itself in an autoimmune disease. I literally started to worry myself to death. I screamed to heaven every day. Not in my time but in God's. Five years later she's coming back and I'm still battling the physical effects of severe worry.

Can you relate? You aren't alone. Most of all, you aren't powerless. Just because you've got eight-legged worry in your life doesn't mean you can't kill it. You can! No matter the size or the number of your worries, you can learn to get in position for God to empower you to battle back worry. If you can, imagine stomping on your health what-if worries. Dead. Imagine God helping you crush the center of your financial what-if worries. Gone. Picture pulling the legs off your marriage or parenting what-if worries. In the pages ahead, you will learn to tear your worries apart with God-given tools and practical application techniques that position you to allow God's power to work in you and through you.

If you picked up this book because you're overwhelmed with worry but aren't sure what you believe about God, read it anyway, even if you haven't settled all of your questions about God. I'm going to tackle worry from a God-centered perspective, but the language and concepts will be explained, so if you're unfamiliar with the Bible, you can follow along. However, if you're a mature believer in God's Word, you'll be sufficiently equipped and challenged to fight like a champion.

While you don't need to be super-spiritual for God to empower you to battle worry, the stronger your tools, the more effective your battle effort will be. Let's say that you're not even sure that you can fight—that's okay. Keep flipping the pages because each page you read is one more foot in the fight. My friend, no matter where you are today, you can learn how to conquer worry.

Yet, I must emphasize that the tools and techniques in this book are energized by God's power. Let me explain: Think about a stand mixer. You can attach the beaters and stir up a cake mix using your own power, without ever plugging the appliance in. *Or* you can plug the cord into the wall and watch the beaters perform with a level of power that you can't create on your own.

That's the difference between trying to battle worry on your own and getting into position for God's power to blast away worry for you. Both situations require that you get into position, but only one allows you to experience exponential power for real and lasting victory. We'll talk about getting into position in chapter 5.

If it's too hard for you to picture yourself defeating worry, that's okay. Don't allow that to turn into a new eight-legged worry. Instead, we're going to follow the journey of someone who had to deal with fears and worries of his own.

Joshua Takes the Reins

Long ago, a man named Joshua was born a slave in Egypt. For hundreds of years, his people, the Israelites, had labored for the Egyptian pharaoh under brutal conditions. Joshua grew up under the hot Egyptian sun, struggling under the oppression of his people's captors, until Moses showed up. As a valiant warrior and Moses's assistant, Joshua spent many years by Moses's side, on the leading edge of danger and uncertainty as they led their people out of Egypt to a land that God had promised them. Finally, after Moses's death, Joshua assumed the top leadership position as God's people prepared to enter their new homeland.

If you've ever started a new job, you can relate to Joshua. As the new leader of the Israelites, Joshua had assumed responsibility for the sustenance and survival of more than a million people and their possessions. Not only that, but God tapped Joshua to lead a military campaign to defeat the inhabitants of their new homeland. Ponder the various fears Joshua might have entertained. Then imagine all of the "what if" worries that accompanied all of those fears:

> *What if the people won't listen to me?*
> *What if I mess up?*
> *What if I'm a failure?*
> *What if our enemies are as big as I remember?*

While we never read a record of Joshua's worries or fears, we know that something was going on in his head because God had to remind him three times to be "strong and courageous" (Joshua 1:6, 7, 9). Furthermore, God commanded him to "not be afraid or discouraged" (v. 9).

Why would God tell a valiant warrior and leader like Joshua not to be afraid or discouraged? Joshua reminds me of Marvel superhero character Captain America, played by actor Chris Evans. Super soldier Steve Rogers, who is later revealed as Captain America, knows who he's fighting for and what he's fighting against. He never confuses the two. As we become familiar with Joshua, we discover that he had the same laser focus. On the battlefield, Joshua led the Israelites to victory, squashing one enemy after another. As Moses's assistant, Joshua was an eyewitness to powerful displays of God's power. Even as Joshua's actions demonstrate that he was a man of great faith, God's command gives us a peek into the deepest recesses of his heart and mind. God

> We all want to be strong and courageous in the face of difficult circumstances, but when we're worried, strength and courage seem to flee.

called Joshua to attend to a shaky, thin place that lay beneath Joshua's military prowess and even his faith.

Notice the first four words God spoke in Joshua 1:9: *This is my command.* Not *Here's a good life lesson* or *This might be helpful for you.* God gave a command, and as a military leader, Joshua understood commands as being directives that brooked no margin for flexibility or negotiation.

My oldest daughter, Kate, is an officer in the United States Army. She's familiar with the concept of commands. In her first moments of boot camp, called Beast Barracks, at the United States Military Academy, my daughter heard a command shouted in the face of every incoming new cadet: "Step up to my line, but not over my line!" My eighteen-year-old daughter knew better than to ask the cadre cadets clarifying questions to see whether they meant to step up at that moment or whenever she was ready. She didn't look around to see what any of the other new cadets were doing. She heard the command and repositioned herself without question and with full attention to the command.

God commanded Joshua to be strong and courageous. Strength is the power to keep hanging on and holding on. Courage is a commitment to act that's bigger than fear. We'll spend some in-depth time together learning how to be strong and courageous. We all want to be strong and courageous in the face of difficult circumstances, but when we're worried, strength and courage seem to flee. How do we learn what it takes to keep fighting without giving up on wayward children, long-term unemployment, an extramarital affair, or chronic illness? Do you have the courage to face the greatest threats to your security? Many of us have the courage to face most things, but do you have the courage to face the hardest, most threatening situations in life, like an unwanted divorce, rebellious children, financial devastation, addiction, life-threatening illness, or persecution for your faith? Courage is facing down a threat. A passion to stand for something greater prevails over that fear.

Let's go back to Joshua 1:9. Even as strength and courage seemed to be Joshua's main vibe, God followed up by naming two postures that will always undermine or short-circuit strength and courage: fear and discouragement.

We've already defined fear as a threat to our security. Fear makes us pause, shrink back, or run away. And as we've already discussed, fear is the birthplace of our eight-legged worry. But did you know that there are actually hundreds of verses in the Bible about not being afraid? Why would God repeat "do not fear" over and over again? He knew we would need reminders at different times and at different places. Neuroscientist Dr. David Rock says, "Your brain is more like a forest than a computer." He meant that, amid constant mental and life change, any qualities or skills that we want to maintain—like fearlessness—will require constant focus and reinforcement or they will evaporate.[1]

God knew that if the fear of our fear was worry, then the best path for His children was to avoid fear. So, God instructed the biblical authors to subtly hit us over the head with hundreds of verses about fear. I love how these verses often pop up in the storylines of those we read about in the Bible.

If you've been run over by fear today, here are a few verses that might encourage you right now (emphasis added):

> Say to those with **fearful** hearts,
>   "Be strong, and **do not fear**,
> for your God is coming to destroy your enemies.
>   He is coming to save you."
>   —Isaiah 35:4

> Don't be **afraid**, for I am with you.
> Don't be discouraged, for I am your God.

> I will strengthen you and help you.
> I will hold you up with my victorious right hand.
> —Isaiah 41:10

> But Jesus spoke to them at once. "Don't be **afraid**," he
> said. "Take courage. I am here!"
> —Matthew 14:27

Do any of these verses speak to your heart in this moment? I hope so! If you are experiencing any worry or anxiety today, I'd like you to choose one of these verses and read it again, aloud if you can. Then I'd like you to close your eyes and imagine God sitting next to you, holding your hand and whispering those words directly to you. If you've always thought of God as someone disappointed or angry with you, try to imagine Him differently. Picture Him as a kind grandfather figure, unhurried and with an easy smile. His warm hand holds yours and you lean against His strong shoulder. God's voice is soft, yet firm, and brings you comfort, perhaps for the first time ever.

If you've never done this before, you might wonder if imagining God like that is okay. It is! While no one has ever seen God face-to-face, the Scriptures tell us all about God's character. He loves you and is always present through every difficulty. Even as God allows circumstances that we wish would go away, He sits beside us through those circumstances and provides comfort and love.

Whatever occupies your mind today, God is sitting with you in that circumstance. He doesn't want you to be afraid, even if you feel that you have every reason to be. God won't abandon you, even in your darkest hour. A pastor named Paul understood this truth and shared a powerful reminder that even if you can't shake your fear or worry, you'll never be able to shake off God's love for you: "And I am convinced that nothing can ever separate us from God's love. Neither death nor life, neither angels nor demons, neither our fears for today nor our worries about tomorrow—not even the powers of hell can separate us from God's love" (Romans 8:38).

Nothing can ever separate you from God's love. Even if you aren't sure who God is to you, He loves you. Even if you've spent your life running the opposite direction from Him, He loves you. Perhaps you're a Christian and you worry that God can't still love you because of what you've done—He loves you. If your hands are shaking while you read this book because your eight-legged worry has ruined your life, your health, your finances, or stolen your hope, nothing can ever, ever separate you from God's love. Nothing.

As we journey along with the man Joshua and the story of the Israelites as they enter their Promised Land, know that the same God who will see them through their ups, downs, and upside downs will see you through whatever you are facing today.

Carry this final thought with you:
God's promises will kill my eight-legged worry.

4

How Do You Stop a Worry?

That the birds of worry and care fly over your head, this you cannot change, but that they build nests in your hair, this you can prevent.

—Chinese proverb

nce upon a time, there was an out-of-control freight train that barreled toward a small town in Pennsylvania, and no one could stop it.

This was the plot behind the 2010 movie *Unstoppable*, starring Denzel Washington and Chris Pine. Washington plays the part of the veteran engineer to Pine's young conductor in this big-budget action movie. The drama begins when a worker forgets to attach the air brake to a train carrying toxic chemicals. At first, the dispatcher believes that the train will just coast through the rail yard but later realizes that the train is running on full power. Washington's and Pine's characters must work through the tensions in their relationship so they can team up to chase down the runaway train in a separate locomotive before the train derails and devastates a community with a toxic chemical spill.

Adding pressure to the tense situation is that the train's speed is increasing over time. As the slow-coasting train gains speed, it evolves into a locomotive bullet charging through rural communities in the quiet countryside.

Throughout the entire movie, the main characters and supporting roles ask the question: How do you stop an out-of-control speeding train?

That's the question many of you are asking about your ever-increasing worry. How *do* you stop unstoppable worry? Maybe in the past, your worry seemed like a harmless, slow-coasting train. When a worry or two popped up, you could stop it without much effort.

But what do you do now that your worry feels like a freight train with a line of cars long enough to make you late for work in the morning, even though you left early? Your worry train feels not only stretched out but also out of control. It barrels back and forth through your mind all day long, and you can't seem to stop it.

When I asked men and women about their experiences with worry, many felt it would be impossible *not* to worry. Most of the intense worriers expressed a level of worry that made them feel powerless to stop it. When we feel powerless to stop worry, then every single concern feels like an out-of-control freight train barreling through our emotions, steamrolling any effort to get a handle on ourselves or our situations.

Like the *Unstoppable* train, your worry-train boxcars are filled with toxic thoughts that threaten to derail your hope, joy, or happiness at any moment. Those toxic thoughts might be contained within your mind, but their fumes leak out and create panic in your heart and poison your peace.

Is it possible to stop your unstoppable worry? Yes, it is.

My friend John is a train conductor near the train yard that the *Unstoppable* movie was based upon. The real-life incident happened on May 15, 2001, when a forty-seven-car train left the CSX yard about twenty miles from my house. As in the movie, two men in a separate engine raced after the train at sixty-five miles per hour. When their engine caught up to the train, they locked the two trains together.[1]

John rolled his eyes a bit when I brought up the movie because while the movie's high-speed storyline made for a great action film, the real-life story behind the movie wasn't nearly as dramatic. So, I asked John if it was possible to stop a high-speed train. His answer provides great insight into how you can find victory over what seems like unstoppable worry.

As the conductor, John builds his train each day by attaching blocks of boxcars to the train's engine. When I asked why we don't see cabooses at the ends of trains anymore, he explained that a caboose was used to carry the flagmen who signaled to ground staff. Once radio and other technology became common, flagmen weren't needed anymore, nor a caboose.

Every train engine and every boxcar is equipped with an air brake hose that keeps the brakes from clamping onto the wheels. As the boxcars link together, one of John's most important jobs is to link the air brakes to each other.

If John ever needs to bring the train to an immediate halt, he can press the emergency brake button. Once that button is pressed, the air hose bursts and the emergency brakes clamp down against engine and boxcar wheels. The brakes arrest the wheels' rotation, and the multimillion-ton train begins to decelerate by way of a long skid. Imagine facing an emergency and knowing that once the brakes are applied, not only do you not have control of the train, but the train is actually uncontrollable until it stops.

Let's look at our worry battle like we're at a train yard. Your mind is the engine, and your "what if" worries are the boxcars attached to your mind. If you had to take a guess, how many boxcars are attached? The longest train on record had 692 cars and was more than four and a half miles long.[2] Thankfully, the train ran through western Australia, so no one got stuck waiting for the train to pass!

If you feel like your worry is unstoppable, is it because you feel you have too many worries? Perhaps you wake up and feel as though new cars have been added to the end of your worry train. A new medical bill arrives, and worries about money tack on another car. You find a suspicious text message on your spouse's phone and you worry if he or she wants to leave you. There's another worry car.

A mind weighted down by worry moves slowly. Proverbs 12:25 says that "worry weighs a person down." It's hard to think about what you actually can do because you're so weighed down by toxic thoughts.

The longer your worry train, the harder it is to bring it to a stop. Maybe this explains why you've been frustrated with your attempts to stop worrying. You've made so many. You've tried to put on the brakes, but your worry train is so long and so filled with toxic thoughts that the entire train feels out of control.

> Jesus wants to know why we're *still* worrying, when we know that it doesn't work.

One of my favorite parts of the conversation with John was this: "Every train can be brought to a stop."

Under normal conditions, John explained, a train needs one and a half miles to stop. That's the length of seventeen football fields. Once the emergency brake button is pressed, the train needs three-quarters of a mile, or the equivalent of eight football fields, to come to a stop.

John went on to tell me a lot of interesting facts about trains, but most important, John reminded me that no matter how fast or unstoppable a train may seem, every train eventually comes to a stop.

The same principle applies to you. No matter how long your worry train, whether two cars or two hundred cars long, you can stop it. And you not only can stop it but also disassemble it and live free in victory and peace.

Every Worry Steals

In Matthew 6, Jesus is preaching His famous Sermon on the Mount. In verse 27, He poses a stunning question that would have stirred the hearts and minds of His listeners: "Can all your worries add a single moment to your life?"

If I had been Jesus, I would have dropped the mic, tossed up a two-finger peace sign, and walked off the stage in search of a comfy chair and a Chick-fil-A sandwich. Jesus knew He had them. People were so obsessed with acting right that they pushed through life with the wrong attitude.

Jesus wasn't just talking to unreligious pagans; rather, He also addressed those in the know. The ones who showed up to church each week, looking spit-shined and spiritual with Sunday Bibles in hand, or at least a YouVersion app downloaded. He was talking to people like us, who had listened to the messages, prayed the prayers, and yet, still worried way more than they should have. Today, Jesus wants to know why we're *still* worrying, when we know that it doesn't work.

He's got us on this one, doesn't He? All of our worries don't add a moment to our lives. But they do add cars to our worry trains and slow us down a little each day. And we think that our worry is working *for* us? Allowing our worry to masquerade as anything other than worry is like pretending our toxin-filled worry train is a hot air balloon.

Notice that Jesus said worry doesn't add a single *moment* to our lives. What are some of your life's favorite moments? Some of my precious moments include the first time my husband kissed me, the day I graduated from college as a young wife and mother, the first time I held each of my children, and the moment I held my first book in my hands. I could write a list of a thousand favorite moments from my life, and not one of them would begin with "the time I worried about

_____."

Worry never adds to our lives; it only takes away. Worry steals our focus from the present. It makes me sad when I think about all the times my children stood before me with a toy or a book, in our warm home on our quiet street with food in the refrigerator and plenty of fresh water in our pipes, and I missed enjoying the moment because I was worried about who would read to my kids if I got hit by a bus and died. In fact, I heaved a big sigh of relief when my youngest child learned to write her name. *I can get hit by a bus and die now*, I remember thinking. For years, I worried about what would happen if I died before each of my girls could write her name. What if they got lost and needed to write a note?! That worry sounds a bit foolish all these years later, but how many moments did that worry steal from my mental and emotional presence in my children's lives? The answer is, a lot.

Have you ever wasted moments worrying when a loved one was diagnosed with a terminal illness? Or fretting about the future as your loved ones longed to connect with your heart? God has given us the "gift of the present"…that we waste in worry about the future.

Every worry-filled boxcar weighing down your mind steals a precious moment from your life. None of us want our precious moments with our friends or families or our free time to be stolen by worry. But how do we get those moments back?

Building a New Train

I love how John explained that his job as a train conductor was to build his train each day. I can see him running the engine into the train yard and picking the track that would hold the boxcars that he wanted to select that day. He had to connect his engine to the boxcars that he wanted to take with him.

If you want to stop your unstoppable worry, it begins with learning how to build your mental train. You've got to learn how to leave the worry boxcars behind and choose wisdom boxcars instead. Wisdom boxcars are filled with God's Word, which breathes life and hope into your present and your future, instead of weighing you down like worry does.

Just as Conductor John received instructions on how to build his train, God gave Joshua instructions on how to build his train of thought so that he wouldn't be derailed as he entered the Promised Land: "Study this Book of Instruction continually. Meditate on it day and night so you will be sure to obey everything written in it. Only then will you prosper and succeed in all you do" (Joshua 1:8).

At the time God imparted this plan for success to Joshua, there wasn't a Bible lying around for Joshua to read each night or flip through in the morning. Rather, Joshua had heard God's laws as recorded by the hand of Moses on tablets of stone. These laws captured God's desired way of life for Joshua and all of the Israelite people. God wanted the people to have a guide for living so that they could choose to live right.

Why would God tell Joshua to study those laws continually and meditate on them day *and* night? Think about your worry train. Does it ever stop running? Mine doesn't. Worries can pop up in my mind at any second on any given day. It seems that God knew this about Joshua as well.

Did you know that 38 percent of people worry every day, most often in the early morning and late at night?[3] That means that at least one out of every three people you know worry about something every day. No wonder so many people are so cranky!

It's the second part of that statistic that caught my attention. People tend to worry early in the morning and late at night. Every morning, we wonder what will happen to us during the day. Every night, we worry about everything that was unresolved. Whatever hasn't been settled or solved becomes a toxic boxcar filled with worst-case scenarios. When I started paying attention to my own habits, I noticed that I tend to experience a surge of worry in the morning as I prepare for the day, and another surge of worried thoughts as I settle into bed at night.

Dr. Caroline Leaf explains what happens to us in the morning and at night: "Daytime thinking is a building process, whereas nighttime thinking is a sorting process." Dr. Leaf is a cognitive neuroscientist who studies how we think. As a Christian, she shares sobering research on why we must pay attention to the toxic train cars that we allow to hook up to our minds: "Research shows that 75 to 98 percent of mental, physical, and behavioral illness comes from one's thought life."[4]

Perhaps this is why God instructed Joshua to read and meditate on His Word before encountering the beginning tasks of each day. Think about what might have weighed on Joshua's mind each morning as he awoke and considered not only the mega-mission of conquering the Promised Land, but also the entire campaign he had to organize as well. Then at night, as Joshua left his leaders and soldiers to settle into his tent for the evening, chances are his mind was filled with what they did, what they didn't, and everything in between. I can just see Joshua lying on his pallet, churning "what if" worries over in his mind. I can see it because I've done it more times than I'd like to admit.

By studying God's Word at the beginning and the end of each day, Joshua could build his mental train and connect God's words of wisdom to the engine of his mind. Worry and wisdom cannot ride together.

This brings up a troubling statistic. According to a survey completed by LifeWay Research, only 19 percent of people who identified a desire to honor Christ in all areas of their lives actually read their Bibles every day. Another 25 percent reported reading their Bibles a few times a week, 14 percent reported reading them once a week, and the final 22 percent read their Bibles just once a month or a few times a month.[5]

If you don't read your Bible every day and now you want to put down the book because you feel bad about it, I'm going to ask you to fight against guilt in favor of contemplating a new thought: *every one Bible verse in has the potential to push one worry out.*

In his observation of nature, meteorologist Edward Norton Lorenz discovered the butterfly effect, the notion that small changes can have large consequences.[6] His research suggests that the flapping of a butterfly's wings has the potential to create a tornado, but the flapping wings are also dependent on all the other emerging conditions that follow. The takeaway for us is that whenever and wherever you position yourself in front of God's Word, it has the potential to accumulate and change your life.

In his book *Growing Strong in the Seasons of Life*, Chuck Swindoll writes about how God's Word changes us: "Your attitudes and outlook will begin to change. Your mind will become alert and observant. Your confidence and assurance will be enhanced. Your faith will be solidified."[7] Your unstoppable worry can be stopped in its tracks when God's Spirit-breathed words invade your life.

If you read your Bible every day and you still don't understand why you're worrying all the time, there's something I'd like you to try called the "God morning/God night" technique. We all want to have a good morning and a good night, but too often worry derails those happy intentions. So, the best way to stop our worry is to crush it with God's wisdom.

Just as those emergency brake hoses are filled with air, we're filled with God's Holy Spirit. When worry strikes, it's the power of God's Holy Spirit that enables us to clamp down on worry and stop it in its tracks. The force of that power depends on how equipped we are with His Word.

First, you'll need a "starter train set." Here are five short verses that can begin your new quest to win your worry battle. Read these verses each morning before you get up and moving each day, and read them before you settle down at night. If you read these verses with the intent to memorize them, eventually they will replace some of the worry boxcars in your mind. The more verses you remember, the more worry boxcars will disappear.

Trust in the Lord with all your heart;
  do not depend on your own understanding.
                    —Proverbs 3:5

When I am afraid,
  I will put my trust in you.
                    —Psalm 56:3

For I can do everything through Christ, who gives me
strength.
                    —Philippians 4:13

Give all your worries and cares to God, for he cares about
you.
                    —1 Peter 5:7

The Lord gives his people strength.
The Lord blesses them with peace.
                    —Psalm 29:11

If you don't bookmark this page, write these verses on two note cards. Leave one card next to your bed, and attach another note card next to your bathroom mirror. Why two? If you oversleep, like me, you might forget to look at the card next to your bed. However, when you brush your teeth, the backup card is right there for you to read.

If you've already memorized these verses, choose five more verses that directly address worry and write them on note cards. We need to give our minds something to connect to each morning before those worry boxcars link up and spread their toxic fumes all over our lives.

Here's a final thought:
Every worry gets stopped in its tracks by the Word of God.

$$\approx 5 \approx$$

Your Three Fighting Friends

Don't show up to a worry battle empty-handed.

—Barb Roose

J never thought that I would jump out of an airplane. My bucket list included taking a yearlong cruise, hiking the Grand Canyon with a can of Raid, and someday selling my house. Skydiving wasn't even on the list of possibilities. Yet, one day I found myself calling 1-800-SKY-DIVE while a roomful of people traded bets on whether or not I'd really go through with it.

Before my hasty decision to jump out of a plane, our church weekend programming team suggested that I touch a tarantula to demonstrate courageous faith. I was preparing a message on Joshua, and they thought capturing me dying of a spider bite on video would be fun.

An image flashed in my mind of me passed out on the ground with the tarantula crawling over me and then into my purse. Then, it crawled back out of my purse, terrifying me again at home that night. My reply was a swift and firm no.

The group brainstormed a number of other possibilities until someone suggested skydiving. I remember thinking that skydiving was my best chance of distracting the team from asking me to touch a spider. I called my husband at work to see if he had any objections to his wife jumping out of a plane the next day. Bless his heart, that wasn't the oddest phone call he's ever gotten from me, so he asked a few questions before giving his blessing. In return, I promised him that I would try my hardest not to die and that I'd be home in time to make dinner.

The next morning, I drove across the state with a producer and a videographer. We didn't say much in the car. I tried to manage all of the "what ifs" going through my mind. *What if the parachute doesn't open? What if I break my leg and can't do my message? What if the plane crashes? What if I don't die when the plane crashes?* The only thing I knew with certainty is that if the plane crashed and I was still alive, my mother would kill me for going skydiving in the first place.

At the jump site, my tandem-jump instructor gave me step-by-step instructions. He told me how to position my body when leaving the plane so that my body wouldn't make contact with the plane on the way out. He stressed the importance of not freaking out while free-falling at 120 miles per hour. The most emphasis came with the landing instructions. To prevent injury, I had to make sure to raise my knees as high as possible before landing so that I wouldn't break my legs.

After the short class, a guy in the staging area was packing parachutes. This was the guy I wanted to talk to, because whatever he was doing would be directly involved in saving my life—and my kids were picky eaters and my husband really didn't like to cook, so I needed to stay alive.

There were three parachutes unfurled and stretched across the floor of the staging area. The parachute pack lay at one end and the actual chute was at the other. In between were the strings. The parachute packer showed me how the parachute worked and then how to pack the canopy into the parachute packs so the strings and canopy would release when the time was right.

How a parachute is packed makes all the difference in whether a jumper has a chance of landing safely or meets disaster. The same goes for our worry battle. Worry is the end result of many circumstances in our lives. But what if we could pack our "parachutes" a little differently? In other words, what if we changed our approach to how we deal with worry on a daily basis?

Introducing Three Fighting Friends

A parachute has three basic parts: the container (backpack), the lines, and the canopy (parachute). Now, of these three, which one is most important to a jumper? All of them! If any of these are missing, the skydiver's experience will be less than favorable.

As we talk about how to approach our worry battle, you're going to meet three new friends. Each of these friends is essential to your worry battle. Each has its own focus and function to get you into position to win over worry. One might feel stronger or more natural than the others, but you need all three. I've found that the fighting friend that I struggle with the most is the one that God uses to help me the most.

Your three fighting friends to help you win over worry are: *peace, courage,* and *strength.*

Peace
Gives you security that soothes your soul.

Courage
Pushes you forward in commitment instead of letting you fall back in the face of fear or worry.

Strength
Empowers you to keep hanging on and holding on.

These three fighting friends are tools guaranteed to put you into position for God to give you victory over worry. These tools are promised to be effective because they are tools divinely given by God to us and for us. In 2 Peter 1:3-4, we're reminded that God never planned for His children to wilt away in worry:

> By his divine power, God has given us everything we need for living a godly life. We have received all of this by coming to know him, the one who called us to himself by means of his marvelous glory and excellence. And because of his glory and excellence, he has given us great and precious promises. These are the promises that enable you to share his divine nature and escape the world's corruption caused by human desires.

Peace is the fighting friend that quiets your mind and assures you of security. It whispers, *God is here. You aren't alone,* even when circumstances around you scream otherwise. When you have *peace,* your mind isn't panicking, your heart isn't racing, and your stomach isn't threatening to erupt. Instead, your mind is calm, your heartbeat is slow and steady, and your stomach is settled.

Philippians 4:6-7 gives you the road map to peace: "Don't worry about anything; instead pray about everything. Tell God what you need, and thank him for all he has done. Then you will experience God's peace, which exceeds anything we can understand. His peace will guard your hearts and minds as you live in Christ Jesus."

What does the Bible mean when it says "Don't worry about anything"? It means don't worry about anything—ever! That feels like crazy, impossible talk for some of you because you can't stop worrying. Perhaps you don't feel like you can stop right now, *but* what if you could take one small step forward? Consider trying the "1+1 technique." One worry = one prayer. If you don't have much experience with prayer or you struggle with what to pray for, begin with this:

> *God, right now I'm scared and unsure what to do.*
> *But I'm bringing all of my worries and giving them to You.*

In this moment, I'm not alone and I choose not to fear.
When I call upon Your name, I know that You are near.

I created this simple rhyme because it's easy to remember. When we're gripped by worry, we don't need sophisticated prayers; we need a simple prayer and a willing heart turned toward God as quickly as possible.

You can get specific about what's going on by following the pattern of Philippians 4:4-6: Pray about it, tell God what you need, and thank Him for what He's done. The best part is that when you do this, your fighting friend of *peace* will show up and calm your head, heart, and stomach so much so that you'll wonder why you're so composed in chaos.

Don't give up on praying because you can't stop worrying. Sometimes we worry, and we feel guilty about worrying. But if you begin with the idea that you're going to pray every time *and* for the same amount of time that you worry, then that's progress!

Imagine a line of peace soldiers with automatic weapons and super-sized cans of Worry Killer standing at the door of your mind. As those giant eight-legged worries start crawling toward your mind, those soldiers blast them with God's peace. Can you see the "what if" legs falling off and then the center of the fear shriveling up and dying? That's the power of God's peace for you.

While your fighting friend *peace* quiets your mind, *courage* is the fighting friend that keeps you from running away from your struggles—even when you really, really want to escape or ignore your troubles.

We all want to envision ourselves as brave enough to run into a burning building to rescue those we love. We want to think we're courageous enough to stand up to bullies. But how do we stand courageous when we're afraid? How do we bravely battle our worry when those same worries seem to bully us?

Courage is when you push forward in the name of what you believe in instead of falling back, giving up, or running away in the face of fear or worry. In many ways, courage is a contradiction. When a house is on fire, we run out of the house to safety. However, courage arises when we run back into the house to bring someone else out to safety. G. K. Chesterton declared that on a certain level courage is "a strong desire to live taking the form of a readiness to die."[1]

Sent by his father to check on his three older brothers, young David showed up on the battlefield as Goliath taunted the Israelite soldiers. David questioned the soldiers who stood by as the nine-foot-tall Philistine giant mocked them and God for forty days. Even as the soldiers ridicule David for questioning their unwillingness to face the giant, he goes to King Saul to tell him that he is willing to fight: "Let no one lose heart on account of this Philistine; your servant will go and fight him" (1 Samuel 17:32 NIV).

David saw that six weeks of taunting had discouraged and demoralized the soldiers. They no longer had the courage to stand up to Goliath. Yet, young David's bravado scaled much larger than his age and size.

When we're worried, the rhythm of our heartbeat sounds a lot like *I-can't, I-can't, I-can't* over and over again. When you're discouraged, you feel your heart sink and your energy drain. After Goliath teased the soldiers and their king, we read, "they were terrified and deeply shaken" (1 Samuel 17:11). Even their leader was afraid to face the giant. But David wasn't.

> There are many times in life when we have more than we can handle. God allows it so that when we realize we can't, then we'll turn toward God because He can!

Courage isn't about winning or losing; it's about showing up and leaning in because it's the right thing to do. Without armor or a sword, young David walked out to Goliath with five small stones, a slingshot,

> When we abandon worry and trust in God, we engage in worship because we are trusting God for who He is and what He will do for us.

and a powerful statement that paints a picture of courage: "You come against me with sword and spear and javelin, but I come against you in the name of the Lord of Heaven's Armies—the God of the armies of Israel, whom you have defied. Today the Lord will conquer you, and I will kill you and cut off your head" (1 Samuel 17:45-46).

David had clarity over the reality he was facing. Goliath was large and well-armed. David was small and had a slingshot. *Underdog* doesn't even begin to describe the scene on the battlefield that day. Yet, David's courageous commitment to God pushed him forward toward his challenge rather than backward, running away.

Your fighting friend *courage* fights for you every time you remember that you aren't alone against worry or challenging situations. Whatever the "giant" in your path, when you remember that you are coming against that worry in the name of the Lord, that giant will fall, and you will have the courage to walk through your battle, not run away from it.

> *You will have the courage to look at that pile of unopened bills.*
> *You will have the courage to keep trying in your marriage.*
> *You will have the courage to go through chemotherapy and radiation.*
> *You will have the courage to let go of a relationship that draws you away from God.*

Our final fighting friend is *strength*. It enables us to keep holding on and hanging on. This fighting friend is different from our human strength, which has its limits. You know that you're at the end of your human strength when you're used up, worn-out, and sucked dry. Our human strength isn't enough to win over worry.

We need our fighting friend, *spiritual strength*. Like *courage, spiritual strength* is a contradiction. Instead of trying to move your mountain of problems on your own, you step back and out of God's way and let Him do the heavy lifting. *Spiritual strength* requires you to give up your I-can-do-it or I-can-handle-it mind-set and tap into a God's-got-this mind-set instead.

If you're still saying, "God won't give me more than I can handle," please stop. Eliminate that phrase from your vocabulary because it will *mess you up*. There are many times in life when we have more than we can handle. God allows it so that when we realize we can't, then we'll turn toward God because He can!

God is able! It's a shame that we're so focused on our worries that we forget just how powerful God really is. The same God who set the sun and moon in the sky knows the exact balance of your checking account. The God who created all of the plants, trees, and flowers also knows how to care for you even if the earthly medicine cannot heal you.

Here's a great reminder for us: "The incredible greatness of God's power for us who believe him...is the same mighty power that raised Christ from the dead and seated him in the place of honor at God's right hand in the heavenly realms" (Ephesians 1:19-20).

God is not sitting in heaven, looking at your life, and saying, "Yikes! She should be flipping out over that." My friend, the same power that God used to raise Jesus from the dead infuses your fighting friends to bring you victory over worry. Those fighting friends don't just help you; they supercharge you to do what you cannot do on your own. This is epic!

As you train your three fighting friends, God will give you victory over worry (Romans 8:37; 1 Corinthians 15:57; and 1 John 5:4). Far too many people, especially Christians, have accepted worry as a way of life. While worry may be a chosen way of life for some, the same God that raised Jesus from the dead will give you victory over every area of your life, including worry! Yet, God doesn't promise us victory just so that we're not panicking every time our teenager goes out for the evening with friends. He makes a promise because of who He is. When we abandon worry and trust in God, we engage in worship because we are trusting God for who He is and what He will do for us.

God knows that when we allow His way of life to flow into our hearts and minds and out through our actions, the resulting transformation testifies to the world of the greatness of God. Your victory over worry is more than just your victory; it is a testimony to God's glory. When you stop fretting and freaking out over stuff or you move from panic to peace, the people around you will take notice. And when you let them know it's because you've learned how to walk in God's promises for your life, that brings God glory.

Now that you've met your three fighting friends, there's one important switch that must be flipped in order for them to go to work on your behalf: you've got to let God lead.

Letting God Lead

After God gave Joshua a personal plan for success and the command to be strong and courageous, it was time for the Israelites to cross over the Jordan River. If you've ever been boating, you know that a lake or river can be pretty wide and pretty deep in places. Now, imagine packing up everything you own and heading down to the nearest river in your community with all of your belongings packed on wooden carts or strapped to the backs of animals.

Imagine our Israelite sister gathering up the last of her possessions as she prepared to cross the Jordan with all of her belongings. Her entire world was about to change in the next few days, but first, she had to risk death crossing over a body of water. I wouldn't blame her if she began worrying, *What if everything gets wet? What if one of the kids drowns? What if we lose one of the animals?*

Our Israelite sister had heard the leaders tell them that the priests were going to bring the ark of the covenant and pass by the people. The people weren't to move until the ark passed by.

The ark of the covenant was a physical symbol of the presence of God.[2] It was often carried before the Israelites into battle, and now, the ark would lead the people across the Jordan and into the Promised Land.

If we drill the leaders' instructions down to a simple one-liner, it would be: *Let God lead.* The people were commanded, "Keep a distance of about two thousand cubits between you and the ark" (Joshua 3:4).

To provide perspective, two thousand cubits—about a half mile— is equivalent to a fifteen-minute walk behind the ark. Such a distance would keep someone from making the fatal mistake that Uzzah made in 2 Samuel 6:6-7 when the oxen stumbled and he reached out to steady the ark.

For me, the distance is also symbolic. Sometimes we get in a hurry when we are trying to get something done. We pray and ask God for help or favor, and at first, we're patient, but when God's taking too long to get us what we want, we are tempted to rush ahead of God.

Joshua told the people to wait for the ark for an important reason. "Then you will know which way to go, since you have never been this way before" (Joshua 3:4 NIV).

> We know that we're rushing ahead of God when we start to worry about details. When we wait on God to lead us, we are far enough back to let God pave the way for us.

We know that we're rushing ahead of God when we start to worry about details. When we wait on God to lead us, we are far enough back to let God pave the way for us.

When we're in the midst of uncertainty, we don't know which way to go. Yet, how often have we run off ahead of God, trying to find our way in the dark, yelling, "It's okay, God. I've got this!"? For me, that usually happens right before I run smack into a wall of worry.

Letting God lead means that we wait for God to move. We *wait*. Even as we're sitting in uncertainty. Even as the WWHMe questions work over our minds. We wait. God likes to make us wait for Him to move. But He makes us wait so that we can watch Him move miraculously in our favor.

Just as the people stayed a half mile behind the ark, so they could see without obstruction God moving before them, we've got to take that step back as well. God is at work in our lives, but if we're too busy trying to run our own agendas, we might be missing *what* He's doing.

You're going to learn much more about training your fighting friends in the next few chapters. But the point isn't to learn about them so that you can go off and fight your worry battle alone. We must let God lead us, both in our uncertainty and in the midst of our worry battle.

Here is today's final thought:
Letting God lead provides clarity in uncertainty.

6

The Cure for "Fast Forgetting"

Anxiety can give you God-Alzheimer's.

—Ann Voskamp

In the 1950s, Ohio housewife Evelyn Ryan needed a solution to keep food on her table and a roof over the heads of her ten children because her husband, Kelly, drank away most of his paycheck each week. In her best-selling memoir, *The Prize Winner of Defiance, Ohio*, Evelyn's daughter, Terry Ryan, described how her mother raised their family by entering advertising contests. In the same way that today's aspiring actors and artists submit YouTube videos to Hollywood or music producers to win contests, mid-century housewives used to create jingles or slogans and submit them to advertisers to win prizes.[1]

Evelyn Ryan brainstormed and wrote jingles and slogans in a spiral notebook that she always left out on the ironing board in the kitchen. Some of her winnings included trips, household appliances, cars, and more. One of her winning entries celebrated spinach, and that jingle won her family a ten-minute shopping spree in the grocery store. That prize was a big deal because Evelyn had so many mouths to feed. If they had medical bills or needed food or clothing, Evelyn sold some of her prizes for cash to take care of her family.

In the mid-1960s, husband Kelly took out a second mortgage on their home without telling Evelyn. A few weeks before they were going to lose that home over a $4,000 debt, Evelyn won top prize in a Dr Pepper contest. She won $3,440.64, as well as a car and a trip overseas.

After her mother's death, Terry went through the stacks of notebooks where her mother had brainstormed jingles, as well as all of the award letters. Terry discovered that Evelyn had won one prize for every four contests that she entered.

While you might have gotten caught up in all the contests and prizes Evelyn won, take a moment and reflect on what was happening around her as she wrote those jingles. Between an alcoholic husband and ten children, what do you think Evelyn would worry about? How could she have the frame of mind to write fun, happy jingles with so much hardship in her life?

Evelyn's story teaches us an important lesson on how to see victory.

In our culture, winning has become defined most often as beating someone or everyone else. Yet, when I read stories like Evelyn Ryan's, I'm reminded that winning isn't just an outcome; it's the symbol of one who has overcome. Winning is overcoming obstacles in our paths, whether it is a person, a situation, or a challenge. The real thrill of victory isn't the accolades but the thrill of getting through or over something in life that you want to leave behind so that you can move forward.

> When we worry, we always assume the next step is disaster. But when we wonder, we believe that our step will eventually take us in a positive direction.

That's why I hate it when I hear someone say, "Oh, I'm just a worrier." Worry has become an obstacle in his or her life. You can characterize worry anyway that you'd like—a black hole, a wall, a mountain, an enemy soldier—but however you picture it, it's blocking you from the thrill of victorious living. The picture of victorious living is the blessing of God's peace, hope, purpose, and joy in your everyday life.

Now, I know that you don't like being a worrier. I'm sure you've tried to fight it. Perhaps you've tried prayer, medicine, counseling, self-help books, positive thinking, talking to friends, drinking, essential oils, exercise—and nothing seems to work. Every time you tried one of those solutions to win over anxiety and worry, the anxiety and worry seemed to win over you. You may not admit this to anyone, but you fear that you're destined to always struggle with worry. But you're taking one more chance by reading this book. (*No pressure, Barb.*)

Here's the thing: I don't feel the pressure to convince you that you can win over worry. I don't feel the pressure because I'm standing on promises! God's promises for victory don't belong to the fastest runner, the smartest student, or the savviest leader. God's promises for victory belong to those who trust in His ability to get them over whatever obstacle or circumstance confronts them.

Before the Israelites took their first step into the Promised Land, God promised them victory over the inhabitants that were already living there. He knew about the giants in the land, as well as the kings who would come out and fight. But God also knew who would be standing in the end. Moses proclaimed to the Israelites as he was preparing them to enter the Promised Land, "For the Lord your God is going with you! He will fight for you against your enemies, and he will give you victory!" (Deuteronomy 20:4).

God was going to not just fight for the Israelites but also give them victory. He would make sure that they were the last men standing when the battle was done. God described what victory would look like for the Israelites in Joshua 1:3-5:

I promise you what I promised Moses: "Wherever you set foot, you will be on land I have given you—from the Negev wilderness in the south to the Lebanon mountains in the north, from the Euphrates River in the east to the Mediterranean Sea in the west, including all the land of the Hittites." No one will be able to stand against you as long as you live. For I will be with you as I was with Moses. I will not fail you or abandon you.

While they stood on the edge of uncertainty, God promised Joshua and the Israelites three types of victory: *personal, provisional,* and *spiritual.* God had tasked Joshua with leading the Israelites and had guaranteed that Joshua would be victorious in what God had called him to do. Then God promised to provide for the Israelites through the land that He gave to them. Even though the land was unknown to them, God knew that land represented a secure place that would provide all of their needs. Finally, God assured spiritual victory as they walked in obedience to His way of life.

You'll notice that there are a lot of locations named—cities, mountains, and rivers—in the above passage. God outlined for Joshua the boundaries of the land the Israelites would conquer. Those boundaries encompassed all of Canaan. That meant that God guaranteed total victory. Only God can assure total victory because only God has total power to ensure it.

But these three areas of victory weren't just for Joshua and the Israelites. God will give you victory in these three areas as well.

Personal
Victory in pursuing and fulfilling your God-given responsibilities in life.

Provisional
Victory over the fear of scarcity or not having enough.

Spiritual

Victory over your carnal human desires that pull you away from God.

Victory over Worry

What would victory over worry look like for you? Is that a question you've ever considered? Here are a few external outcomes associated with victory over worry:

- dealing with an unexpected mechanic's bill without tears or terror, even though you aren't sure how to pay the bill
- managing your career without obsessing about who might be talking behind your back or plotting to sabotage you
- going to bed and actually sleeping, even though your adult child has been making poor decisions
- surrendering your circumstances to God instead of succumbing to an unhealthy habit when feeling worried or stressed

Before we can experience a victorious outcome, we must start with reprogramming our inner thoughts. Your mind is just like a portable hard drive or cloud storage account. What you store in your mind stays in storage until you recall it or recycle it. Every worry is a file uploaded to your mind. Likewise, every Scripture verse, song, or experience with God is uploaded as well.

If you think about your brain, how many worried thoughts, fears, or flashbacks are stored in your mind? A lot of smart scientists talk about how flashbacks to negative events or traumas actually cause individuals to relive those events over and over in their minds until they begin to see the world only through their trauma.[2] However, we can overcome worry, anxiety, and flashbacks through our God-given fighting friends, who help us access God's power to overcome and live victorious.

Even as science offers us insight from our human perspective, God actually revealed this truth to us long ago: "Fix your thoughts on what is true, and honorable, and right, and pure, and lovely, and admirable. Think about things that are excellent and worthy of praise.... Then the God of peace will be with you" (Philippians 4:8-9).

In the previous chapter, we talked about building a new train with Scripture verses to use throughout our day. Now we're going to explore how to store memory files of God's presence in our lives for the future. This is similar to what God told Joshua and the Israelites to do as they embarked upon the Jordan River crossing.

The God Who Makes a Way

When we last left our Israelite friend, she was waiting for the ark of the covenant to pass by so that she and the millions of other Israelites could follow. Can you picture her checking her family tent to make sure that everyone had on his or her sandals? I wouldn't be surprised if she threatened to leave her ten-year-old daughter behind if she didn't change her attitude. *Girl, don't make me leave you on this side of the river!*

I can see our friend struggling to stay focused on the matters at hand, yet straining to look off into the distance for any clues about what would happen next. As she saw the priests and the ark moving toward the Jordan without a boat, lots of questions about how she would get her family safely across would have started percolating in her mind.

Now, Joshua told the people that the next day God would perform more great wonders before them. Did the people go to bed with the same anticipation as a child on Christmas morning, or did they suffer a sleepless night like someone waiting for medical test results?

Do you tend to worry or wonder? Author Dan Zadra says, "Worry is a misuse of the imagination."[3] Worry is thinking of all the ways that something might go wrong, but wonder anticipates a smorgasbord of positive possibilities.

My friend Braelee suffers from social anxiety disorder. While we were in Honduras recently, she told me about her journey to deal with her anxiety and how she took a big leap of faith to spend six weeks overseas. One of the events that shaped her faith happened after she unexpectedly lost a job. Braelee didn't understand why her position was eliminated, and the loss upset her. Then she interviewed for a position at the church, but didn't get the job. Another setback. However, Braelee said that she began to focus on all the times God had provided for her in the past. She stayed calm and watched for other opportunities. Eventually a job opened up that allowed her to cover her monthly expenses, as well as participate in the paid apprenticeship program.[4]

When we worry, we always assume the next step is disaster. But when we wonder, we believe that our step will eventually take us in a positive direction.

After the priests passed by, our Israelite friend grabbed her children's hands and followed behind. She remembered what we should never forget: *to let God lead.* Soon she and her family began the trek toward the river.

Now, our friend had likely visited the Jordan River for water while the Israelites camped, so as she approached its banks, chances are that our sister anticipated wet kids and wet bedding, and possibly even worried about the loss of one of the kids or, at the least, some of her possessions (like a few animals). But when the river came into view, she noticed something quite stunning: the waters were pushed far back and the riverbed was dry—not muddy, but bone dry.

As the Israelites walked on a dry riverbed across the width of the Jordan River, they had to pass by the priests, who stood with the ark in the middle of the river. It was a reminder that God had not only performed a miracle and held back the waters of the river but, if they waited for Him, would also *always* make a way where there seemed to be no way.

"Fast Forgetting"

I'm a fast forgetter. I tend to quickly forget God's blessings that I should remember, yet I also tend to forget the pain that accompanies some of my poor life choices.

A few years ago, I discovered that I could no longer eat fried fish, coleslaw, and New England clam chowder at the same time. You might not care about this combo, but it is delicious. I believe that heaven will serve this meal as the nighttime snack after the wedding feast of the Lamb (Revelation 19:9). If you check out Jesus's miracles, you will see that He was partial to fish. (After His resurrection, He cooked fish for the disciples.)

While I will definitely enjoy fried fish, creamy coleslaw, and creamy soup in heaven, I must remember never, ever to eat it on earth together again. Unfortunately, it took three different, yet equally miserable nights of clutching random hotel toilet bowls (emptying myself of all that was within me) for me to realize that I needed to let those items go from my life.

Not only do I forget about foods that I cannot tolerate; if I'm not careful, I'm quick to forget the record of God's blessing in my life. Yet when I remember, I relax. When I reflect on what God has done, then I can refocus from *What will happen to me?* to *God, I know that You will give me victory!*

God understands that we are all fast forgetters. Likewise, God knows that fast forgetting is what leads to our fear in the first place. Forgetting what God has done for us leads to fear when uncertainty strikes. Marking the moment and maintaining our memories of God's past victories not only cures fast forgetting but also reconnects us to God's promise to give us future victory.

God demonstrated this when He instructed Joshua to pick one man from each of the twelve tribes to choose a large stone from the area where the ark was positioned in the riverbed. The twelve men carried their large stones on their shoulders to where the Israelites set up camp at Gilgal, on the other side of the river. This is what Joshua told the people: "We will use these stones to build a memorial. In the future your children will ask you, 'What do these stones mean? Then you can tell them, 'They remind us that the Jordan River stopped flowing when the Ark of the Lord's Covenant went across.' These stones will stand as a memorial along the people of Israel forever" (Joshua 4:6-7).

Not only did they build a memorial at the camp, but Joshua also set up another pile of twelve stones where the ark stood in the middle of the dry riverbed.

God told the Israelites that He would do great wonders before them that day, and He did. God pushed back the Jordan and dried the riverbed so the Israelites could walk safely across. Not only that, but there were no enemy kings waiting on the other side to attack them.

As amazing as God's demonstration of power was that day, God knew that the Israelites were fast forgetters. They'd proved that over and over again while traipsing around the desert. Yet, God still ordered them to create a memorial that would stand and remind them of what happened that day because He knew that they would eventually forget.

Creating Your Own Twelve Stones for the Future

If you think about your life, do you have any tangible reminders of how God has made a way for you through difficulty and hardship?

On a recent trip, I stayed with my friend Kathy. As she showed me around her house, Kathy pointed out family heirlooms and photos. Yet her proudest possession was a small bookcase stuffed with thirty years of prayer journals. These notebooks contained memories of God's faithfulness during all the years of Kathy's spiritual journey, her husband's illness and young death, the ups and downs of single parenting, and the trials and triumphs of life along the way. That bookcase is a tangible memorial of her life with God. Kathy says that she goes to that bookcase whenever she needs encouragement because, like Braelee, she knows that the God who was faithful to her before will always be faithful to her in uncertainty.

As I read the story of the twelve stones, God challenged me to create a new memorial with twelve specific memories of His faithfulness. I had many years of journals, but recently I discovered that I must have thrown them out. Yikes! Now God has given me an opportunity to create a new memorial, a scrapbook with only twelve pictures. Scrapbooking can be overwhelming because there's so much to choose from, but this idea is specific and hopefully not as intimidating as trying to do one of your entire life. However, I did meet a man who, in my opinion, is the best scrapbooker I've ever met. I stayed with Craig and his lovely wife, Sandi, while in Des Moines for a speaking engagement. He's an engineer with a construction company, but his hobby is creating stunning scrapbooks of the annual vacations they take with another couple. As I flipped through more than a dozen four-inch-deep albums, their memories, beautifully arranged, brought me to tears. And I'd just met them! Shared memories are powerful! Craig's museum-worthy memory book includes clip art, captions, and beautiful photos taken by his childhood friend. Here's the thing about Craig and his scrapbooks: he completes them in less than two weeks. Incredible! But it won't take you as long. I promise!

Here's what I did: I made a list of twelve times when God showed up and made a way in my life when there was no way. Then I took that list and found photos of that time in my life. If I couldn't find a photo of the specific event, I found one of me during that time in my life. Finally, I placed the photo on a scrapbook page and added a clipping of the story from that situation. At the beginning of the book, I put the verse from Joshua 4:21, and I wrote Joshua 4:24 on the final page: "He did all this so that the nations of the earth might know that the Lord's hand

is powerful, and so that you might fear the Lord your God forever."
Perhaps you might like to do this as well. I've posted a few pages
of my journal on Pinterest, and you're invited to share yours with me.

If scrapbooking isn't your thing, you can also collect twelve stones,
big enough to write on the bottom. Use a marker or label to write your
twelve memories on the stones, and place them in a beautiful bowl or
glass-bottom dish.

Whether you create a scrapbook or write on stones, what's most
important is to keep these memories where you can see them often.
Keeping them visible might also invite visitors to ask about them,
allowing you to share God's faithfulness. You never know who God
might use you to encourage!

As I reflect on the men who created the stone memorial, I know
that it didn't happen instantly. The men had to wrestle the rocks onto
their shoulders and then carry them to camp. They had to arrange the
twelve stones so that they would not topple over. Afterward, I'm fairly
sure that our Israelite sister brought her children over to the memorial
and bent low to explain why that memorial existed. As she told the
story and admonished her children to never forget what God had done,
our friend probably prayed that she would never forget as well.

Unfortunately, we do forget. We get busy. We get stressed. We get
worried. But when we've created a memorial, we give ourselves a great
gift: a chance to remember.

We remember how God has done great wonders in our lives.

We remember how He made a way when there was no way.

We remember God's love and power exhibited for us.

As Ann Voskamp says, "When we remember how He blesses, loves us,
when we recollect His goodnesses to us—our broken places *re-collect*.
We re-member. We heal."[5]

~ 7 ~

When You Can't See Around Your Situation

When your life feels like it is falling apart, hang onto Jesus!

—Barb Roose

While our Israelite friend set up camp for her family after crossing the Jordan, another woman, named Rahab, was living a short distance away in the city of Jericho. She'd heard rumors about a large group of wanderers close by, but she couldn't see them because she lived behind Jericho's giant wall.

The city of Jericho, known as the City of Palm Trees, is considered the oldest continuously inhabited city in human history. Jericho's location in the Jordan Valley meant that its tropical climate produced crops like date palms, bananas, and lots of other types of tropical fruits. Since they couldn't grow anything in the dessert, Israelites had been eating manna each day for forty years. The prospect of fresh fruit and other foods native to that area would have perked up a few palates.[1]

Jericho was the first city on Joshua's military strategic plan to conquer in the Promised Land. The Israelite camp at Gilgal is located a short distance away from Jericho. Before crossing the Jordan, Joshua sent out two spies to check out the city of Jericho and provide a report when they returned.

Rahab lived behind Jericho's stone wall with a few thousand people in the city. The city was built on a mound, or "tell," with a stone wall around its base. Then there was a retaining wall, like what you use around your patio or garden, that was between twelve and fifteen feet high and about six feet thick. A second wall atop the retaining wall stood another twenty to twenty-six feet high.[2] If you're keeping track of the math, the walls of Jericho during Rahab's time were between thirty-two and forty-one feet tall. If walls could talk, Jericho's wall shouted, "Built to last longer than you."

It wasn't uncommon for cities during that time to fortify themselves with walls. To discourage wandering raiders and to maintain a military advantage against another army, a city's wall provided both offensive and defensive benefits.

Would you feel safe living inside those walls of Jericho? They were really big walls. Seems like they could have kept out a lot of potential problems. However, walls that big could also block out good things too.

Do you have a worry in your life right now that feels like a giant wall with no way over it? Worry walls represent obstacles in our lives that cause us to feel stress and anxiety because we can't move forward or get ahead.

What are the worry walls in your life right now?

Uncertainty in Life

If you don't know Rahab's story, she was the kind of woman most of us are quick to look down upon because we like to judge people by what we see. What I love most about Rahab's story is that she wasn't the picture of the perfect Christian who says and does all the right things. She was actually far from it! But Rahab's life is proof that you can face uncertainty with faith over fear or worry.

In Joshua 2:1, Rahab is described as "a prostitute." When we first meet her, we also discover that the two spies Joshua had sent to scout Jericho had ended up at her home, which was, again, built into one of Jericho's giant walls. That's important; we'll come back to that.

These days, we recognize that women involved in sex work are usually victims of kidnapping, abuse, or slavery. In ancient times, women had few means of supporting themselves without a father or husband. In fact, "poverty was by far the most common cause of prostitution in the ancient world, as it is in our world as well."[3] Such a perspective helps us view Rahab's situation and motives through a different lens.

In Joshua 2:2, we're given another important piece of information. Someone had told the king of Jericho that there were two spies within the city walls—and that they were staying with Rahab! I love how the Bible says, "Someone told the king." Someone is always starting something! This tells us that the people inside the walls of Jericho knew about the Israelite camp at Gilgal. They didn't need social media to move information around.

The king sent Rahab a message telling her to bring out the spies who were hiding in her home. Common sense says that a prostitute might angle for special favor with the king by turning over the spies at his request. After all, a woman of her station in life has limited opportunities for the future. But Rahab didn't turn over the spies.

For Christians, what Rahab did next would create serious tension, but it also created important dialogue, as well. The tension: Rahab lied to the king. How can God celebrate someone who lies? That's what I love about the people we read about in the Bible! The pages of Scripture are filled with imperfect people who feared, fell, lied, cheated, and stole. Yet, when some of those people allowed God into their lives, He changed them from the inside out. The problem for us is that we like to judge people by what they've done in the past instead of by who they've become once they allow God to transform their lives. When you read the Bible and encounter people like Rahab, remember that God isn't calling you to model their lives; rather, you can model their faith.

Rahab didn't just tell a lie. She created a whopper of a story that would make a sixteen-year-old caught staying out past curfew proud. And it worked! The king's soldiers took off to the mountains, where she'd said the spies had gone, in hopes of capturing them before they made it back to the Israelite camp.

Later that night, Rahab went up to the roof of her home, where she'd hidden the spies under stalks of flax that were drying. She engaged the spies in conversation and revealed precious words of wisdom we can use to help us tear down our worry walls, beginning with the first phrase she spoke to them: "I know the Lord has given you…" (Joshua 2:9).

Those words are a mirror reflection of God's promise to Joshua. Rahab was living behind Jericho's walls when Moses taught the Israelites what God promised from the eastern side of the Jordan River. She didn't see God push back the waters of the river, nor did she walk across the dry riverbed. Yet somehow Rahab knew God's promises and she believed them. Not only that, but Rahab gave the spies a history lesson of the Israelites' conquests over other kings. That's a lot of knowledge for a woman who lived behind a wall.

Here's our first lesson from Rahab on letting God deal with our worry walls: *even when you can't see what's beyond your current situation, God is still God.* We can't know everything, but God does. Even if we knew everything, that doesn't mean that we could do anything about it. However, God knows everything, and He's powerful enough to do anything! After Rahab told the spies that the people living in Jericho had lost courage, she explained why: "For the Lord your God is the supreme God of the heavens above and the earth below" (Joshua 2:11).

How many times have our worries about the future led us to questions about God? We ask, "God, are You there?" or "God, why is this happening to me?" or "God, do You even love me?" Perhaps you feel trapped, and things in your life seem to be slipping out of control. There was a season in my life that I call "the Dark Years." I was stuck behind a giant worry wall, with tarantula-sized eight-legged worries keeping me up at night, and causing anxiety and meltdowns all day. I was a Christian, but because I was stuck, I began to question God's love for me. I kept asking, "God, why are You letting all of this happen to me?"

You might be familiar with a man named Job in the Bible who lost everything, including his home, his children, his health, and his faith. In the midst of his story is a stretch of chapters in which God speaks directly to Job to address his question, "Why me, God?" Here's part of God's answer:

> Where does light come from,
> and where does darkness go?
> Can you take each to its home?
> Do you know how to get there?
> But of course you know all this!
> For you were born before it was all created,
> and you are so very experienced!
> —Job 38:19-21

When I read God's response to Job, I realized that God never answered why Job was facing the uncertainty and painful circumstances in his life. Honestly, my first thought was, *That's rude.* Job had asked God a question that we all ask, so why didn't God answer? Instead, in Job 38–41, God asked Job dozens of questions that reminded him that God's knowledge, power, and presence far exceed our narrow human perspective.

God invites us to come to Him with our uncertainty, but that doesn't mean that He owes us an answer. And consider this: even if

God gave you all of the answers, is that what you really wanted? No—what you really want is security.

Answers aren't security. God is.

God finished His declaration to Job with a question that stills my heart every time I read it: "You are God's critic, but do you have the answers?" (Job 40:2).

I can hear the mic drop in heaven after God spoke those words. The truth is that I don't have the answers, and walls in my life remind me that I don't. They also remind me that I may not always have a place to go, but I always have a God to go to.

God's Got This

After the king's soldier left Rahab's home, she asked the spies to protect her family as she'd protected them from the king. Specifically, she asked them for a "sure sign" that her family's life would be spared. Rahab had no guarantee that the men would help her, but she had the courage to ask. Had Rahab been wrapped up in worry, she would have missed her opportunity to ask for help. This leads to the second lesson we can learn from this prostitute: *don't let your panic cause you to pass up an opportunity to ask God for help in faith!*

"Many seek the Hand of God but...few seek His face," the saying goes.[4] This quote means that we often want God to rescue us, but we don't want to have a relationship with Him. In ancient times, people did not have access to God as we enjoy now through our relationship with Christ, but Rahab demonstrated that her request for help was because she no longer associated herself with the people of Jericho. She followed Israel's God, and she didn't want to suffer the punishment of those who didn't want to follow that God.

The spies agreed to Rahab's request, and before they left her home, they told her that their agreement would not be binding unless she met their conditions: "When we come into the land, you must leave this scarlet rope hanging from the window through which you let us down" (Joshua 2:18).

Here's where things get interesting. The spies left, and all Rahab had was a red rope hanging out of her window and a promise. She was still living behind that wall, and she had no idea what would happen next.

The toughest part about the worry walls in our lives is that we have to wait for God to come rescue us. Just like I couldn't climb over the Warrior Dash wall on my own, we can't climb over our worry walls on our own; we have to wait for God to move us over whatever is blocking our way.

Imagine what it must have been like for Rahab and her family as they waited inside her home each day for something to happen. We know that the spies hid out for at least three days before returning back to the Israelite camp. Then there were seven days when the Israelites marched around the walls of Jericho before God showed His power and plan.

Who loves waiting? Not me. But it's in the waiting where we learn the third and most important lesson from Rahab on how to deal with a worry wall: *when your life feels like it is falling apart, hang on to Jesus!*

For all of those days of waiting, Rahab could have decided that she wanted to create her own solution because God wasn't moving fast enough to help her. But she didn't.

What about you? Have you ever faced a seemingly impossible situation and decided to create your own solution instead of waiting on God? Unfortunately, I have an advanced degree in this kind of foolishness. Once, when my house wasn't selling, but I really wanted to buy the house up the street, I bought that house anyway...without telling my husband.

Your worry wall can become God's way of showing you His power. He allows situations to surface in our lives that we can't get around so that we'll turn toward Him. God likes to show off. We know this just by looking at the world around us. Rainbows, lightning, sunsets, the northern lights, mountain ranges, and flowers all testify to God's extravagant power demonstrated for our pleasure. There are times when God wants us to witness His outrageous power to build our faith.

During that dark season of my life, one of my children needed a medical test that the school requested, but our insurance company wouldn't cover it. The out-of-pocket cost was staggering for our family budget. The name on my worry wall was my child's health and welfare. There seemed to be nothing I could do, and my inability to effect change brought me to my knees in my kitchen. Of course, the difficulty with the test wasn't the only situation on our plates at the time.

For most of us, a worry wall isn't usually the only issue in our lives. However, it is the issue that gets our focus and attention because it's the only one that we can't push through. When we hit a situation that we can't push through, our frustration builds, not just because of the situation itself but because of our inability to change it.

While down on my kitchen floor, I shook my fist toward heaven and said, "God, why aren't You doing something about this?" Tears flowed down my face, and I just wanted to give up. I even thought about walking away from my faith because what good was following God if He wasn't going to help me? But then I realized that walking away from God would leave me to handle my worries all on my own. It was at that point that I raised my eyes toward heaven and surrendered. I gave up. I stopped trying to move a wall that only God could move. It was then that I said, "If it's gonna get done, God, You are going to have to do it."

A few minutes later, my phone rang. It was an office assistant from my children's school. She said, "Mrs. Roose, I didn't know if you knew this, but there is a fund here at the school that can cover the cost of the test that your daughter needs."

God did it! He didn't need my help. In fact, that day is one of my twelve memorial stone days because God showed up and moved a wall that only He could move. That was never my wall to move—it was His.

Hanging on to Jesus

What could it look like for you to hang on to Jesus when you're behind a wall in life that won't move?

There's a little more to Rahab's story that we'll cover in the next chapter, but let's take a moment and focus on that scarlet rope hanging from her window. There are many people, places, events, and objects in the Old Testament that symbolize God's relationship with humanity in the New Testament. This rope is one of them.

Rahab's scarlet rope is a symbol of salvation. Some scholars suggest that it was the same rope that the spies used to escape; others discount that possibility, noting that two different Hebrew words are used. In either case, the scarlet rope in the window served as a reminder each day that salvation was coming. It's no mistake that it was a scarlet rope, as it mirrors the blood of Christ's sacrifice for us, which made the way for our salvation. Eternal security is our most desperately needed security of all.

God's promise to save us encompasses both our eternity and our everyday lives. So, when you're faced with a situation that makes you feel trapped or as if your life is falling down, remember to hang on to Jesus.

What does it look like to hang on to Jesus? For me, it's clinging to Jesus like a two-year-old who doesn't want to go into the church nursery. Not only does that little kid have a suction-cup grip on his or her mother, but that little cherub looks dead center into mama's eyes with a look that says, "Don't let me go!"

For me, hanging on to Jesus begins when I choose Jesus in uncertain times instead of trying to figure everything else out myself. I also cling to Jesus when I feel I'm emotionally or spiritually falling apart. I actually call out, "Jesus, I'm hanging on to You!"

I also find wearing a reminder bracelet helpful during high-stress times. I have a "Jesus, I'm hanging on to You" bracelet that I literally grab with my hand whenever I need it and say, "Jesus, in this moment, I'm hanging on to You." I don't know about you, but when I'm really stressed, my prayers are not fancy or sophisticated. My brain isn't working all that well, but I can say those few words.

Perhaps you might want to try out the "Jesus, I'm hanging on to You" technique by getting a bracelet or a red piece of string and putting it on your wrist. For seven days, hold on to it whenever you get scared or worried and pray the following prayer: "Jesus, in this moment, I'm hanging on to You. I know that You're here with me, and You're going to get me through this."

When I do this exercise, there is something comforting about grabbing onto a physical symbol that reminds me of Jesus. There's nothing supernatural about the bracelet. It's just a symbol. But something supernatural does happen anytime you reach out to God in prayer.

As I've done with the Twelve Stone memory book, I've included some pictures on Pinterest of bracelets that you can make on your own.

As we leave Rahab's story, I'm reminded that
when I wait for God to tear down my worry wall,
I'll always be amazed at how He takes care of it all!

~∞ **8** ∞~

Circumcision of the Heart

A person with a changed heart seeks praise from God,
not from people.

—Romans 2:29

hile Rahab waited at home within the walls of Jericho, our
Israelite sister and the rest of the community settled in to
a new camp in their new land. Can you see her trying to
figure out where to unpack her household and warning her kids, "Yes,
you can look around our new neighborhood, but don't get lost!"? As
if walking through the dry Jordan riverbed weren't enough for one
day, God had two more blessings waiting for them on the other side:
renewal for the future and a release from their past.

It had been forty years since the Israelites had regularly observed
their commitment ritual of circumcision to God, but now that they'd
arrived, it was time to reconvene that ritual.

Many marriage renewals are inspired after a couple overcomes
a significant marriage event, whether a near divorce, a separation,
or a health crisis. Other couples renew their marriage vows as they
celebrate milestone anniversaries, such as the tenth, the twentieth, or
the twenty-fifth.

There were no fancy dresses or five-course dinners during God's renewal ceremony of circumcision, though there were some sharp knives involved. Circumcision was the sign of the covenant between God and Abraham. The Hebrew word for "covenant" is "betweenness." A covenant is an agreement between two people or two groups that involve promises from each to the other.

In Genesis, God promised the childless Abraham that He would bless his descendants and make them God's special people. God would take care of them and fight for them against their enemies. In return, Abraham would remain faithful to God and abandon worshiping other gods, as had been the way of his ancestors. The sign of that covenant was circumcision. It was after Abraham's circumcision that his barren wife, Sarah, became pregnant.

For generations, Hebrew males were circumcised as part of the covenant. But the wilderness years brought that covenant activity to a halt, not just because they were wandering around a dusty desert but also because they rebelled. Remember, it was only supposed to take eleven days for the Israelites to reach Canaan after leaving Egypt. But when God gave the Israelites the permission to enter, they rejected God's provision out of fear. For their rebellion, "the Lord vowed he would not let them enter the land he had sworn to give" (Joshua 5:6).

Since they broke their agreement with God, He withdrew the right for the adults at the time to enter the Promised Land. In fact, the Israelites wandered the desert until everyone over the age of twenty at the time of the rebellion died. Only two people over that age survived: Joshua and a man named Caleb. These two men begged the people to follow God into their blessing, but the people rejected God out of worry and fear. Not only did the Israelite adults lose their blessing, but they spent every day trudging through the wilderness, burdened by regret. Fear and worry cost them their future.

Our Israelite sister would have seen her parents perish in the wilderness. I imagine that she heard them voice their sadness, regret, and maybe even bitterness over their fear-driven rebellion. To know that their actions had caused their children to spend their lifetimes as wanderers must have been a difficult burden to bear.

When I ask people to identify those in their lives who constantly express worry, the answer is *their parents*. One woman recounted her struggles with her mother's constant worry, and now she realizes that her mother's worries are even more influential than she thought. "What bothers me the most is her irrational worries are starting to rub off on my kids. I hate that her worries cause them now to worry about irrational fears."

A cautionary note for those who will influence the lives of the next generation: if fear and worry control your life today, then you risk subjecting those you influence to the outcomes and consequences of your worry for many tomorrows.

Circumcision of the Heart

God wanted to renew His covenant with a new generation, so Joshua circumcised the new generation of men who represented their families. While a discussion about physical circumcision can feel a little awkward, the Bible also talks about a more important, even more personal type of circumcision that applies to all of our spiritual conditions: circumcision of our hearts.

In the New Testament, the debate over circumcision created a lot of bad feelings between Jewish believers and Gentile believers. Although both groups had accepted Jesus Christ through faith, there was a segment of Jewish believers, called *Judaizers*, who wanted Gentiles to be circumcised before being accepted into Christian community. These were people who showed up early to church every Sunday looking good and smelling good yet judged everyone else who didn't look or talk Christian enough. You don't know any Christians like that, right?

Judaizers created division in the church, and the apostle Paul had to step in to provide some pushback against their insistence on following Jewish rules: "No, a true Jew is one whose heart is right with God. And true circumcision is not merely obeying the letter of the law; rather, it is a change of heart produced by the Spirit. And a person with a changed heart seeks praise from God, not from people" (Romans 2:29).

Circumcision of the heart is a description of how the Holy Spirit reshapes our hearts by cutting out what keeps us from enjoying and protecting our relationship with God. If we know that God is the source of our peace, courage, and strength, then that should motivate us to ask God to cut away whatever gets in the way of our connection to Him. This means that fear and worry must be cut out of our lives so we can enjoy a connection with God. This also means that any sin must be identified and surrendered as well.

Perhaps you've realized that God is leading you through a circumcision of the heart right now. Have you been trying to deal with your worry so that you could appear to be cooler and calmer under pressure, or do you really want God to change the way you think, feel, and act? As you consider where you need God to circumcise your heart, know that it's a process that we all undergo in every step of our Christian journey. And circumcision of the heart is a lot more challenging than just following a bunch of rules.

So many Christians want just enough of God to look good to everyone around them. This is why Christians love rules. Go to church on Sunday. Check. Wear a skirt that comes down to your knees. Check. Don't indulge in any of the three M's (booty-shaking music, secular movies, and malt beverages). Check.

We want to know who's in the club versus who is not. If someone can follow the rules, then we'll let her sit at our cool kid table on Sunday mornings, but if she doesn't know all the rules, we won't tell her. We'll just show off in front of her and then shame her until she gets it right.

Perhaps you are struggling with your worry battle because you've created a secret list of rules for your Christianity. These are the rules to help you look like you are a really good Christian. Or maybe you don't have any of your own rules, but you've been trying to live up to someone else's.

I grew up with a "look good on the outside" mind-set. I took pride in the fact that I was a good Christian kid. I didn't get in trouble. I was nice to my teacher. I didn't roll my skirt up once I left my home, and I didn't ditch church. But my heart suffocated under the burden of rules to keep me looking good on the outside. I struggled with myself on the inside, and even worse, I judged people who struggled on the outside.

I had a list of secret rules that governed my late teens and well into my late twenties. If I had to write them down, they would look like this:

1. I have to be good if I want God to love me.
2. I can never let up on trying harder.
3. I always have to look like I've got it all together.
4. I can't tell people when I feel weak or like a failure.

What are your secret rules? Mine left me tied up in knots about my relationship with God. *Would I ever be good enough for God? What could I expect from Him?* That kind of anxiety sapped my enthusiasm for studying my Bible because instead of wondering what God wanted from me, I worried about making sure that no one ever had reason to call me a bad kid.

However, I had my own wilderness rebellion in college. I decided I wanted to take a break from being good. I even prayed and told God about it. This is true! I said, "God, I've been a good kid all of my life, but now I want to go and have some fun. So, help me not do anything stupid or kill myself."

For a while, I refused God permission to circumcise my heart. One of the clues of an uncircumcised heart is the unwillingness to pray. I also stopped reading my Bible. Even though I knew that blocking God out wasn't best for me, I still did it.

I'll never justify my rebellion, but the consequences of that time in my life showed me what God's grace truly looked like. As I look back through the eyes of compassion, I can see how it was born out of the foolish rules that I placed upon myself to look like a good Christian instead of allowing myself to enjoy the grace and love of a good God.

Once I realized that God didn't need me to live by a list of rules, I was free from worrying about being a good Christian, and I could celebrate the fact that I was God's daughter. That's a much better place to be!

God Chisels the Heart

As I connect with God as His daughter, He gently leads me away from the heart attitudes that threaten our relationship...like worry. Over the years, God has led me through my desert dark years that felt like they'd never end. He taught me about gratitude during that season of my life. I've crossed a few "Jordan Rivers" that taught me about dependence on God instead of trusting in only my talents and abilities. For the past few years, God has led me through the challenge of uncertainty. I left a full-time staff ministry position at a large church to go into solo ministry. There was a stretch in time when my relationship with my husband teetered precariously on the edge.

In all these places, God has allowed these circumstances to challenge and chisel away at the fears and worries in my heart to make more room for Him in my life. The more I clung to God through those times, the more fear and worry fell away.

Where do you need to give God permission to circumcise your heart? What secret rules, bad attitudes, fears, and worries need to be cut away? What does a circumcised heart look like? One thing is for sure, it's not a perfect heart. But it is a willing heart. Here are three indicators of a circumcised heart:

1. A willing heart is eager to worship.
2. A willing heart loves Jesus and His imperfect people.
3. A willing heart trusts God at His Word.

God's not going to cut away anything that He's promised to you, but you might miss out on it if you choose to cling to fear and worry. Can you trust God's gentle hand to move you away from what's hurting you and toward healing?

The beauty of the gospel is that it continues to unfold in our lives each and every day of our lives if we let it.

When I made it through that one dark year period of my life, there was a thrill in seeing God in a brand-new way. I enjoyed a deeper sense of faith because I'd seen God make a way for us where there was no way. Instead of fast forgetting, I worked hard to remember His faithfulness at all times. But then something else unexpected happened. Once I got to the other side, I began to beat myself up for my lack of faith during those years. As I walked in a new rhythm of faith and less stressful circumstances, I reflected on my former self with disdain and even some shame. *Why did I freak out over the car engine? What was wrong with me? Why did I get so stressed over the emergency room visit? Why didn't I keep it together when my husband and I faced that problem?*

> The beauty of the gospel is that it continues to unfold in our lives each and every day of our lives if we let it.

When we look back on certain seasons of our lives, it's easy to beat ourselves up for our mistakes or shortcomings. We might also beat ourselves up because we weren't equipped to handle the circumstances or the consequences of circumstances in front of us. Yet God sees that our struggles are just part of the process.

C. S. Lewis brings such compassion to our worry battle. He wrote, "Some people feel guilty about their anxieties and regard them as a defect of faith. I don't agree at all. They are afflictions, not sins. Like all afflictions, they are, if we can take them, our share in the Passion of Christ."[1]

When I think about our Israelite friend, I wonder how her worldview was affected by not only her parents' rebellion but also the knowledge that her people were enslaved only a generation before. Life in Egypt was difficult, not just because of Pharaoh's harsh treatment but also because of the mental, emotional, and spiritual impact of slavery. The Israelites were captive physically, but they were also captive to the criticism from those who taunted Israel for being slaves.

As an African American, I don't know much about my ancestors' years in slavery. There are very few written records and even fewer photos. However, many generations later, I still can see the mental and emotional consequences of slavery passed down through our family line. Not everyone has carried the consequences the same way. Some family members remember our enslaved ancestors as brave, courageous people and seek to model that strong, proud heritage. Others reflect on slavery with bitterness and anger, particularly if parts of their lives feel enslaved today. The feelings associated with shame, injustice, missed opportunities, delayed reward, and victimization can be passed down through the generations like a family name.

God did not want the new generation of Israelites moving into the Promised Land with old shame and regret. After the covenant with God was renewed, God announced another renewal: "Today I have rolled away the shame of your slavery in Egypt" (Joshua 5:9).

On the Sunday morning after Jesus's crucifixion, Mary Magdalene and Mary the mother of James went to anoint Jesus's body in the tomb. The women questioned who would roll away the large stone blocking the entrance because the religious leaders wanted to make sure that no one came to steal Jesus's body after His death. However, when the women arrived, the large stone had already been rolled away. (See Mark 16.) Setting the stone in place was the final step in the death phase of Jesus's mission on earth. He was betrayed, beaten, tried, convicted, crucified, and buried before a large stone sealed the end of that part of His mission. Nothing could move forward until that stone was removed. Yet when the stone was rolled away, everything that had been done to Jesus was overcome through God's power that brought Jesus back to life.

Rolling away can be viewed as what was in the past no longer having the power to ruin our hope for a future. God rolled away the shame of the Israelites' captivity, as well as their rebellion, so they could walk forward into God's Promised Land confident in His promises. They didn't have to worry about whether or not God would hold their past against them.

For us, when we allow God's Spirit to circumcise our hearts, He leads us through a process of confession, repentance, and acceptance of His forgiveness. This process rolls away the sin or guilt from our lives and allows us to experience the sweetness of freedom. Furthermore, as we move through the process of allowing God to battle our worry for us, we don't allow ourselves to get discouraged by what we used to do or what we failed to do. We celebrate by giving thanks to God for what He is doing and for His Spirit working in us and through us. The Scriptures tell us that "wherever the Spirit of the Lord is, there is freedom" (2 Corinthians 3:17).

To commemorate God's removal of the shame of their captivity, Joshua called the place where the Israelites camped "Gilgal," which means "rolled away." For the people who lived in the camp at that time, they were no longer the descendants of slaves. Rather, they reclaimed their right to become children of God. That makes a difference when you wake up and look at yourself in the mirror each morning!

One final event occurred after the circumcision and God's removal of their shame. The Israelites partook in the Passover meal for the first time since leaving Mt. Sinai (Numbers 9:5). Since this group of Israelites, camped at Gilgal, were young, they would have never prepared this symbolic meal.

Imagine the solemn awe when the men selected a lamb from their flocks as a sacrificial substitute for their families' sin. Now picture the women gathering the bitter herbs to commemorate the years of slavery and baking the bread that reminded them of their ancestors leaving Egypt in a hurry.

I wonder if our Israelite sister shared stories with her children that were shared with her from her parents and grandparents about their time in Egypt and their escape. I'd like to think that this time she told those stories with hope in her heart for the future.

Is it time for you to give God a chance to circumcise your heart? Whether you've never done this before or it's been a long time since you've done it, is today the day that you need to confess an uncircumcised heart? Have you been unwilling to let God in because you've been off doing your own thing?

Here's a suggestion for you: If you are willing, make a list of fears, worries, secret rules, and wrong attitudes that need to change. I did this exercise many years ago and it was so powerful and freeing for me. Here is what you need to do:

1. Write each of your fears, worries, secret rules, and wrong attitudes on a little slip of paper.
2. Tell God about each of them. If you need words for your prayer, you can use these:

> Dear God, thank You for wanting to be in a relationship with me. God, I am so grateful that You sent Jesus to die for my sins so that I can enjoy a relationship with You instead of having to follow a bunch of rules.

God, I want to tell you about _____
_____. This is a part of my life that keeps me
from getting close to You. God, You have permission to remove
it from my life. I give permission to Your Holy Spirit to change
my heart so that I can draw closer with You. I reject any feelings
of shame or any whispers of lies because I know that I am Your
daughter and You love me.

3. After you pray this prayer, rip up the slips of paper and put the pieces
into a fireproof bowl or container. At the end of your time of talking
to God, you can burn those little bits of paper carefully until they are
no more.

4. If you can, journal about your experience or a take a few photos to
mark the moment. Write down how it felt to write out all of those
slips of paper and then to ask God to forgive you or roll away your
shame. Make sure to capture how you feel when the exercise is over
and record any questions that you might have too. God may use this
experience to begin a new season of your life that might contain a
little uncertainty, but that's okay!

Just as the Israelites shared their memories during their Passover
dinner, you can come back to the memory of this day when you need a
reminder in the future.

Let's finish with this final thought:
*Moving forward often means that we have to let God cut away our
unhealthy heart ties to the past.*

∾ 9 ∾

God, If . . .

If God is for us, who can ever be against us?

—Romans 8:31

*I*n January 2012, I had just finished speaking at a women's conference in La Ceiba, Honduras. For two days, hundreds of women gathered to learn, connect, and worship together at a church positioned on top of a hill with the beautiful Caribbean Ocean in the background. Within two hours of returning to where I was staying, I was hiding under a bed with my dear friend and host, Aurora, and another friend, Diana, as rapid-fire and automatic weapons erupted in the neighborhood.

As the bullets bounced around us, I remember hearing footsteps running by and around the house. As we tucked our bodies farther under the bed, I reached for my iPad and sent a message to my husband. Not wanting to upset him with the details, I kept the message short and just let him know that there was trouble. While grateful for Wi-Fi to communicate, I wondered if that would be the last message I sent to my husband. What if someone tried to break into the house? What if they fired bullets into the house?

The aftermath of that day was horrible and tragic. Many lives were lost that afternoon in that quiet neighborhood, including one of the church's talented young worship leaders, Brian Rosales. He had been walking down the street to meet up with a friend before afternoon music practice. I'd had a brief conversation with Brian after church fewer than twenty-four hours before. Now he was gone.

While I was present for the tragic events of the day, the tragedy didn't directly impact my life. Yet, I struggled with the effects of the incident for several months to come. When I returned home, I had difficulty sleeping and nightmares for several weeks. Even though I knew that it was normal to struggle, I felt guilty about not wanting to return to Honduras, a place I considered my second home.

For weeks that tragic afternoon replayed in my mind all day and kept me up at night. You can believe that I called on all of my fighting friends, because I needed help. Rather than fight to keep the memories from my mind, I let them in and then surrendered them to Jesus. *I can't fight these on my own. I'm giving them over to You, Jesus.* As 2 Corinthians 10:5 says, "We demolish arguments and every pretension that sets itself up against the knowledge of God, and we take captive every thought to make it obedient to Christ" (NIV).

In my mind, the battle raged over what I'd experienced and the fears and worries about that same experience in the future. I couldn't fight those thoughts off on my own, but when I let them in and kept challenging them with the power of God's Word, those memories lost their power in my life.

As I worked through my struggle, I could see my friends in La Ceiba also heal from the tragedy. Not only had the church's attendance doubled, but television stations all over the country picked up the tragic story and Brian's testimony was shared throughout the country for God's glory.

It took about eighteen months for me to return to Honduras, and I've been many times since. That community of believers is family to me. I didn't want fear or worry to keep me from staying connected with them. When my mind began to wander into "what if," I used prayer tools like 1+1 and meditated on lots of Scripture.

Returning to Honduras was a victory for me! I knew that God was calling me back and that God would "have my back." Furthermore, the reward of embracing my Honduran family was worth every bit of battle I faced and overcame in Jesus's name.

Staying connected to God's presence in times of great stress or worry is difficult. Letting go of control and leaving the outcome up to God isn't easy either. When we're under pressure, we tend to shift our focus from God to whatever needs to get done. Joshua ran into this problem as he prepared for the Israelites' first battle against Jericho. God sent a unique messenger to help Joshua refocus.

Whose Side Are You On?

After the Passover, Joshua left the camp and was near Jericho. It's not hard to imagine a brilliant leader such as Joshua doing his own surveillance work, checking out the wall or counting the number of enemy soldiers he could see. Did Joshua feel the tension between God's promise of victory and his soldiers' lack of weapons? Perhaps he was looking for the signs of panic that Rahab had told the spies about and that they would have reported to Joshua when they returned to camp. Whatever Joshua's actual thoughts, he surely had a lot on his mind.

As Joshua was walking down the road, a man with a sword stood in front of him. We don't know if Joshua possessed a weapon of his own. But he did fire off a direct question: "Are you friend or foe?" (Joshua 5:13).

Joshua's question seems to parallel the mentality of our culture today. Have you ever felt some anxiety before posting on social media because you're afraid of offending someone? We've divided ourselves along the lines of pro-life versus pro-choice, Republican versus Democrat, and so on. We want to know who is on our side and who isn't. When Pastor Rick Warren was asked if he was left-wing or right-wing, he answered that he was neither. "I'm for the whole bird!"[1]

Since the day of battle was coming, Joshua wanted to know if the man in his path was for or against him. I love the man's answer: "Neither."

As a military man, Joshua must have been surprised to hear a man carrying a sword claim neutrality when war was on the horizon. But the man wasn't neutral. Instead, he was there to provide the essential clarity that Joshua needed before commencing battle. He answered Joshua with an introduction: "I am the commander of the Lord's army" (5:14).

Who was this man, really? Some commentators believe the man was a theophany, or an appearance of God as a man, or perhaps a Christophany, which is a pre–New Testament appearance of Christ.[2]

Does the man's response mean that God wasn't on Joshua's side? If God wasn't on Joshua's side, then all of His promises were no longer valid. Clearly, God wasn't against Joshua. So, what was the man's message? God wanted to remind Joshua that he was fighting on the almighty God's side and not the other way around.

Joshua may have been a valiant warrior and leader, but the Promised Land campaign wasn't his battle. It was God's battle.

When God fights for us, He doesn't need our help. How often do we strike out to try to fix a situation thinking that God is on our side, but we fail to ask whether or not our attitude or action is on God's side? Joshua modeled the attitude that positions us to experience God's victory. After the Lord's commander spoke, Joshua replied: "I am at your command. What do you want your servant to do?" (5:14b).

In that moment, Joshua surrendered his plans and submitted his leadership and influence to the direction and authority of God. Once Joshua surrendered his agenda, he was ready to follow God's plan for victory.

Just so Joshua never forgot that the Promised Land was a special blessing from God and not just a military battleground, the man told

Joshua to take off his sandals. This was an act of reverence. It was not Joshua's battlefield that they were standing on. It was God's place of battle, which made it holy ground. God had already told the Israelites many times that He was going to give them the land, so the battle was God's to fight.

Whatever battle you are fighting right now isn't actually your battle. And yet, how many of these statements sound like you?

- "I've got to save my marriage."
- "I need to get my kid back on track."
- "I have to work three jobs, seven days a week, to get my money right again."
- "I need to fix my relationship with my coworker."

Of course you need to get involved in these situations, but these battles are God's to win.

When the Israelites fled the Egyptians, Joshua was on the run too. He would have been in the crowd as they looked toward the Red Sea and felt trapped by the water on one side and the deadly warriors bearing down on them on the other. You might say that the people were flipping out! In that perilous moment Moses told the crowd, "The Lord himself will fight for you. Just stay calm" (Exodus 14:14).

Do you realize that God invites us to be calm even when we don't see a solution because He's going to provide the solution for us? After Moses spoke, God opened up the Rea Sea, not just so the Israelites could pass through, but so their enemies would be defeated. But staying calm and leaving the outcome up to God isn't easy, is it?

God, if . . .

Picture Jesus in the Garden of Gethsemane, the olive grove where He took three of His closest disciples, Peter, James, and John, on the night He would be betrayed. Jesus knew that it was time for God's redemptive plan to move forward, meaning that Jesus would face physical beatings and pain before dying a humiliating death on a criminal's cross. Matthew 26 records Jesus's prayer to God on two separate occasions: "My Father! If it is possible, let this cup of suffering be taken away from me. Yet, I want your will to be done, not mine" (verse 39). A few verses later, Jesus cried out again: "My Father! If this cup cannot be taken away unless I drink it, your will be done" (verse 42).

I think it's meaningful that Jesus prayed the same prayer twice. Notice how both prayers began with "My Father! If..." Rather than run through the frightening possibilities of what was to come, Jesus leaned in toward God. While He expressed anguish over His circumstance, Jesus didn't abandon His commitment. He didn't run away. Jesus shows us that courage and commitment begin with "God, if..." instead of worry-affirming "What if...?"

How many times have you wished you could just run away from your worries? If you've got eight-legged worries about your family, friends, finances, health, or politics chasing you day and night, it's no surprise that you're tempted to do as the song says: "I want to get away, I want to fly away."[3]

Maybe running away isn't your problem, but you feel paralyzed. Worry has profoundly crushed any move forward. You've got so many eight-legged worries running around your mind that you can't clear away the cobwebs to make wise decisions. So, you do nothing. Your worries get worse, but you're trapped into believing that nothing can change or nothing you do will make a difference.

Switching from "What if..." to "God, if..." flips us from fear to faith. When you look at the challenges in front of you and say, "God, if...," that changes your focus from believing that everything relies on you to everything—including the outcome—rests in the capable hands of a loving and powerful God. You may not be able escape the difficult situation, but you'll have the peace, courage, and strength to remember that you aren't alone.

How would you handle it if you and your friends were facing death for refusing to pledge allegiance to a god you didn't believe in? In the Old Testament, three young men—Shadrach, Meshach, and Abednego—opposed the king's command to bow down to a golden statue, much to the anger of the king, who'd trained and promoted them up the ranks of the Babylonian kingdom. When they refused to bow down, the king sentenced them to death in a fiery furnace. We wouldn't have blamed the young men if they'd developed a case of eight-legged worry. These young men could have bowed down to the idol to escape death or leveraged some of their power to flee the country. Instead, they found their courage in "God, if" rather than panicking over "what if...?": "If we are thrown into the blazing furnace, the God whom we serve is able to save us. He will rescue us from your power, Your Majesty. But even if he doesn't, we want to make it clear to you, Your Majesty, that we will never serve your gods or worship the gold statue you have set up" (Daniel 3:17-18).

Notice that their "if" didn't have legs of worry and disaster. Rather, it was tied to a security that God was in control of their lives. Rather than trust in their power and influence, they committed to God, and that commitment was even greater than their fear of death.

Like Joshua, Jesus, and the three young Hebrew men, when we surrender ourselves to "God, if" instead of writhing over "what if," we transfer our hope to God instead of our own self-effort. As God says, "It is not by force nor by strength, but by my Spirit" (Zechariah 4:6).

Too often, we picture surrender as giving up on something. We don't like to give up because that feels like failure. But what if we could "give over"? What's the difference? Giving up is the loss of hope, but giving over is the transference of hope.

God's got a solution to your predicament. Is it time for you to get out of His way? How can you know it's time for you to give over your problem to God? Here are three indicators:

1. You realize that all of your best efforts, including time and money, aren't enough for real lasting change.
2. You are trying to change another person's behavior (that is, "fix" him or her).
3. Your attempts leave you feeling drained, disappointed, or damaged.

Surrendering to God's Success

Giving ourselves over to God is also called "surrender." In fact, surrender is a form of self-control. Knowing what is our role and what is God's responsibility can save us a lot of struggle and worry. Spiritual surrender looks like the same attitude that Joshua displayed when he said to the commander of the Lord's army, "I am your servant. What do you want me to do?" (Joshua 5:14, paraphrased).

Joshua knew that if he was to be successful in what God had called him to do, then he would have to surrender his heart, mind, body, and soul to God's direction. Obediently following after God is the essence of surrender.

A psalmist used deer as a powerful illustration of the kind of passion we should have for following God: "As the deer longs for streams of water, so I long for you, O God. I thirst for God, the living God. When can I go and stand before him?" (Psalm 42:1-2).

Deer will walk long distances for water because there's nothing that quenches thirst like water. Jesus talked with a woman who'd made a lot of questionable life choices because she was looking all in the wrong places to quench her thirst for love, affection, and connection. He offered her "living water," but she had to surrender her life to Him in order to experience the full satisfaction of what He had to offer (John 4:10).

What about you? I'm not sure where you are spiritually today. If you've already accepted Jesus Christ as your Savior, then is there any part of your life un-surrendered to Him? Chances are this is the place where you're trying to fight worry on your own. If you haven't accepted Jesus, are you ready to give up on trying to fix your life and accept God's help? If that is your desire, then you can pray this with me:

Dear God, I'm tired of fighting life's battles on my own. Today I surrender my heart, mind, body, and soul to You. Thank You for sending Jesus to die on the cross for me. He surrendered His life to Your will so that I could experience victory here on earth, as well as eternal victory. Help me understand what it means to love, trust, and obey Your ways. In Jesus's name, amen.

If you surrendered your life to God for the first time, then you've activated God's power in your life! Reach out to a trusted Christian friend and share this with him or her. And feel free to send me an email so I can be praying for you!

Here's one final thought for this chapter:
Surrender isn't a sign of failure; it's a powerful step of faith!

10

God, Knock Down My Worry Walls

Give it to God and go to sleep.

—Anonymous

*H*ave you ever sensed God leading you to do something that made absolutely no sense at all? Maybe you felt Him nudging you to pray for someone or stop by and visit someone. Perhaps you've strongly sensed that you should text someone to see how he or she is doing. In those moments, you wonder if it really matters if you follow through or not.

One Sunday, I spent a long afternoon on a layover at O'Hare airport after teaching at a women's retreat in the beautiful Keweenaw Peninsula of upper Michigan. I wandered around the airport for a half hour looking for a comfortable spot to spend the next six hours. I circled the terminal multiple times, testing and rejecting different resting locations. At one point I felt like Goldilocks. *This spot is too far away from the bathroom. This spot doesn't have any power outlets. This spot is too far from Starbucks.*

I settled into a location that was near the bathroom and plenty of power outlets. A family with four little girls tumbled into the row of seats behind me. Even as my headphones dampened their chatter, I could still hear the dad coaxing and calming them. Within moments, I could tell that their pit stop was unplanned and the family was very uneasy about their situation. As the dad talked on the phone, I couldn't help overhearing him say things like, "Their passport cards won't be accepted" and "We're thinking about splitting the family up."

I took off my headphones and asked, "Is there anything I can do to help?" He smiled, relaxing a face that seemed like it had been tense for a long time. The dad explained that his family was traveling to visit relatives in Canada, but there were issues with two of his four children's passports. He was talking with his wife about him taking two kids and traveling by car and her taking the two with the problem-free passports and traveling by plane. Plane travel became a problem because the cost of the tickets jumped to more than $1,000 per person.

In that moment, I felt helpless. There was a real and present need in front of me, but I didn't have the power to effect change. However, I could pray and I could invite others to as well. I pulled out my phone and typed a quick message to folks on social media, inviting them to pray for this little family.

Within a few minutes of our chat, his wife showed up and the dad left to try to work out a solution with the airline. I went back to working and continued to pray for God to show up. An hour or so had passed when the dad returned with a shocked look on his face. "They gave us the last six tickets on that flight," he rasped, with watery eyes. "And they didn't charge us a thing."

I grabbed my phone as he hugged his wife. I showed them the social media post and the comments of people who had prayed for them. If you've ever had this type of moment, you know there are no words to describe what it means to be a bystander and watch God at work. I couldn't do anything tangible in that circumstance, but through prayer, a group of us petitioned God to act on the family's behalf.

Move that wall!

When a physical wall is built, the builders mean for it to last. No one builds a wall with the expectation that it's going to randomly fall down on its own. When we see walls fall down, there's usually some catastrophic force from the outside or a slow, insidious decay from the inside.

The most shocking physical walls that I've ever seen come down were the walls of the Twin Towers on 9/11. If you were watching television that day, you'd agree that there are few words to describe what it was like to watch something so strong, so formidable, tumble down.

> God's greatest work within us and around us often happens when we get out of our own way.

The walls of Jericho were built to keep the city safe. The gates were the only vulnerable spot in Jericho's wall, so those gates were tightly shut to keep residents in and to keep everyone else out.

When I think about my giant wall of worry, I see two little French peas perched on top. Perhaps you've seen those little peas in the *VeggieTales* episode "Josh and the Big Wall." They liked to sing a sweet, smack-talking song to the Israelites walking around their city. The little peas find it absurd that the Israelites think walking will bring down the walls.

> It's plain to see your brains are very small
> To think walking will be knocking down our wall.[1]

Know this my friends: God specializes in taking down walls that keep His children from claiming their promises. In fact, before Jericho's walls ever came down, He reminded Joshua, "I have given you Jericho, its king and all its strong warriors" (Joshua 6:2). Every institution that made Jericho strong was going to be subdued and given to the Israelites under God's power.

This is where things get interesting for Joshua and the Israelites. If you had been an Israelite soldier, you'd probably be wondering exactly how you were going to take possession of a city that's behind a wall that's too tall, too thick, and too strong to climb over, dig under, or hammer down. That's the wall that the Israelites couldn't bring down on their own, and they couldn't get around. Yet God gave Joshua the instructions for how to bring down the wall.

> You and your fighting men should march around the town once a day for six days.... On the seventh day you are to march around the town seven times, with the priests blowing the horns. When you hear the priest give one long blast on the rams' horns, have all the people shout as loud as they can. Then the walls of the town will collapse, and the people can charge straight into the town. (Joshua 6:3-5)

Wait... *what*?

And not only did God tell the men to walk and not fight, but Joshua gave them one more command: "Do not shout; do not even talk.... Not a single word from any of you until I tell you to shout. Then shout!" (Joshua 6:10).

I don't watch many of those gladiator-type movies. It's hard to follow the story line with all of those muscles getting in the way, but from the ones I've seen, I've noticed that there are two things that warriors like to do: fight and yell. Yet, the Israelite soldiers were instructed to do the exact opposite. What about that strength-and-courage speech God had given Joshua? Seriously, how much strength and courage does it take to walk around a wall and be quiet?

When we have a problem, we usually envision how we think it should be solved. If we pray about our problem, then we also envision the way God should handle it too. There is a powerful passage of

Scripture in Isaiah 55:8 that summarizes God's unique response to the challenges we face in our lives. He says, "My thoughts are nothing like your thoughts... and my ways are far beyond anything you could imagine."

Silence Is Golden

God's never going to take down a wall in your life the way you want Him to. He's going to deal with that wall in a way that is best for you. Could it be that God is waiting for us to get silent before telling us what to do while waiting for Him to move? We might find out that when we stop talking, we're better able to see what God is already doing instead of running around trying to help God out.

Have you considered that the wall in your life may not need you to attack it? If you are facing a wall of financial debt, what would it look like for you to step back from hustling three jobs or borrowing money to pay back money? Yes, you need to open all the past-due envelopes and create a plan to reduce the debt. But do you believe that God can create ways for you to pay down the debt without you resorting to measures requiring you to miss church every week or never have time to attend a Bible study?

Perhaps you're facing a health crisis and you've tried every treatment, medication, essential oil, and relaxation technique. If you are tired, discouraged, and struggling under marital strain, have you sensed God whispering for you to step back because He's got a different way to solve your situation?

Sweet friends, I'm all about due diligence and hard work. However, when we're constantly pushing against something that isn't moving, could God be sending us a message to stop what we're doing and give Him a chance?

God's greatest work within us and around us often happens when we get out of our own way.

Think about how it felt as the Israelite soldiers marched once around the wall each day—in silence. It would have been hard not to cash in on their adrenaline by thumping each other on the back or trash-talking the Jericho soldiers watching from above. *We're coming for you!* Keeping quiet also meant that they would have to keep their worries to themselves about whether or not they thought Joshua's instructions from God would actually work. *Wouldn't it be faster for us to just fight? And why didn't God snap His fingers and take the wall down like He split the Jordan River?*

Whenever I'm looking at a worry wall in my life, I want God to show up and take it down with guns blazing. I want to see fire from heaven and angels swinging sledgehammers attacking my massive issue until the wall tumbles into rubble. While there are times when I've experienced the miraculous, instantaneous movement of God, it's rare. Most of the time God uses my worry wall to teach me about Him. As I've learned how to battle worry, I've discovered that part of God's plan is to teach me how to be obedient to His transformation process.

When it comes to worry walls, the first principle that I keep in mind is that I don't need to wear myself out by doing too much. Instead of trying to outhustle God in my situation, I'm learning to walk in the balance captured in this quote attributed to Saint Augustine: "Pray as if it all depends on God. Work as if it all depends on you." The question I challenge myself with is: *Have I devoted as much time to praying as I have to planning or doing?* Prayer is doing something. In fact, prayer is also key to keeping you from doing other, unproductive things.

One of the kids accidently broke a windowpane on our back kitchen door. My husband put up a temporary piece of wood, and I was frustrated because I just wanted him to fix the glass. My "what if" worries fired up, and I began to feel annoyed and anxious over our safety if my husband didn't get around to the repair immediately. Then I remembered to pray and felt God telling me to stop worrying and to not do or say anything.

The next day, my husband asked me if I'd looked at the back door. I hadn't checked, and he smiled. The door was fixed. The night before, he had found a replacement piece of glass in the basement, pried out all of the glazing and wood, and replaced the broken pane. God didn't need me to nag or try to do it myself. Shocking, right?

Walk by Faith

The second principle I keep in mind when facing a worry wall comes from the example of the Israelite soldiers walking behind the ark of the covenant. Those fighting men were literally walking by faith. God told them what to do and they did it—not knowing what God would do. Hebrews 11:30 records the acts of these men generations later, "It was by faith that the people of Israel marched around Jericho for seven days, and the walls came crashing down."

They didn't know what God would do; they just knew they had to walk by faith and wait for God to do something. Now, at some point, those soldiers must have felt silly walking around that wall. I can imagine Jericho's soldiers tossing rotten food or other things since the Israelite soldiers were passively parading, not attacking. But they kept walking until God told them what to do next.

I remember when God told me that it was time to leave my full-time job at my church. It was December 2014 when I first felt God's leading. By August 2015, I'd been on staff for almost fourteen years, yet I could no longer manage the load of working a challenging job for a megachurch, writing books, speaking, and traveling. Not only did my family suffer, but I was struggling. However, I didn't know how I could possibly leave my job.

> The difference between worry and worship is who you're talking to.

But that's what God was calling me to walk toward. For the next four months, I walked by faith without all of the answers. We had to organize our family finances, like making new budgets and saving a lot of money. I remember buying several pairs of shoes one month because I didn't think I'd be able to buy shoes after my income dropped.

As I walked by faith, God showed me the way one step at a time. I didn't know how to manage what felt like a wall of uncertainty, but God walked me through it day by day. When I challenged myself to worship God by taking my questions about the future directly to Him instead of worrying about how to deal with the future on my own, I grew in my faith in God. Walking by faith was my role while God broke down my wall.

What does walking by faith look like for you?

If you're facing a situation right now, what would it look like for you to see it as an opportunity to worship God for who He is rather than worry about what you're going to do? The difference between worry and worship is who you're talking to.

Be Still and Know

The last and most difficult principle to embrace while learning about letting God tear down my worry wall is a spiritual discipline that God's sons and daughters need to practice more often in today's world: silence. Richard Foster, author of the classic *Celebration of the Disciplines*, defines *silence* as not just the absence of speech, but the presence of active listening.[2] Therefore the discipline of silence is to learn how to see and hear.

Thanks to today's technology, we can tell anyone and everyone about our problems. As women, we've got a lot of words at our disposal. The only time we're speechless is when our kids clean up their rooms without us asking, right? We use our words to text people, label sad selfies on Instagram, write a "Prayers needed" status on social media, create a blog post, or even send a good old-fashioned email. If it's really serious, we might even consider calling someone on the phone, but that's only in the direst of situations. (Sarcasm intended here because a growing percentage of us are actually alarmed when our phones ring.)

Many years ago, my husband sent me on a silent retreat because I had begun suffering from stress-related short-term memory loss. My nerves were perched on pins and needles twenty-four hours a day. I couldn't relax or remember anything, but I obsessed over everything. That sweet man found a retreat center about an hour away from our home, pressed some money into my hands, and told me to go.

Let me give you a heads-up on something: when you're stressed out, silence is horrible. I thought I would lose my mind the first few hours. I've never done drugs, but I felt like my mind and spirit were detoxing from constant noise. I couldn't sit still, and I felt nervous and jittery.

My room at the retreat center was stripped of anything that could distract me from just being with myself. There was nothing for me to plan, file, buy, cook, clean, pay, or manage. It was just me. And I hated it. In fact, I left my room looking for something to do so I wouldn't have to be by myself. I was so desperate to find something to do that I went for a walk and ended up in a cemetery adjoining the retreat center property. I was so excited to see that cemetery! As I walked up and down the rows, I read the gravestones of nuns who belonged to the order that supported the retreat center. I wondered if it was easy for them to embrace the silence that often accompanied their life.

> When we see God getting ready to do something, the excitement is often too big for us to behold.

It took an entire day for me to settle down and let the silence surround me. Stillness is a strange but welcomed sensation when you finally stop avoiding it. I think about the Israelite soldiers as they marched around the walls of Jericho and the only sound was the rhythmic crunch of marching feet. At some point those soldiers must have stopped thinking about the wall and instead started thinking about the walls that kept them from a deep and abiding relationship with God.

How do you know that you need to incorporate silence into your life? Here are three clues:

1. You always feel that you must be doing something.
2. You are uncomfortable or afraid of silence.
3. You can't stop your mind from racing.

If any of this sounds like you, then you need to lean into the discipline of silence.

It can be an uncomfortable feeling to sit in the silence with yourself. For me, when I sit with myself long enough, I discover that the real wall that needs attention isn't the situation in front of me, but usually the walls within me. Silence forces me to listen for my heartbeat and reckon with the sound of my heartache.

If you want to begin incorporating silence into your life to give God space to deal with your worry walls, try the "seven minutes of silence" technique. The next time you feel compelled to pick up the phone to call someone and complain or express your worries, grab your phone and set the timer for seven minutes. Then sit on your phone. Yes, sit on it so you can't see it or any notifications that might pop up on it. Warning: this will be tough because a flood of thoughts and emotions will overwhelm you, but sit strong. If you can only make it a few seconds or a minute at first, that's great! Just keep doing it until you learn to embrace silence once a day. This teaches us to trust that we don't need to be doing something every second and to wait on God to do what only He can do in our lives.

CRASH!

And the walls came crashing down . . .

You probably already know the end of the Jericho story. Yes, the walls came crashing down. On the seventh day, God told the Israelites to march seven times around the city walls. I'm sure that the people within the walls wet their pants once the Israelites circled that wall a second time on the seventh day. Conversely, imagine the excitement and anticipation of the Israelites as they circled the wall those seven times. When we see God getting ready to do something, the excitement is often too big for us to behold.

The moment finally came when the trumpets blared and the people shouted. The blast of their verbal roar must have been heard far beyond Jericho. As those walls began to shake, split, and tumble down, I can see our Israelite sister staring in awe and wonder. God has left me speechless like that at certain times in my life—like when my university couldn't process my financial aid forms and I had no way to pay for school. It was a wall that I couldn't move. Yet when I was called into the bursar's office, the official interviewed me and asked about my GPA and class activities. Then, based on my GPA, he gave me a tuition payment extension so I could stay in school. The extension expired the day my financial aid came through. That wall fell, and I was speechless.

I don't know what wall you are facing today, but I hope that you consider those three principles of not doing too much, walking by faith, and practicing silence.

When it comes to your worry walls, here is a final thought:
God knows how to get us through whatever walls that He does or does not take down in our lives.

11

In Case of a Meltdown . . .

If you treat every situation as a life or death matter, you'll die a lot of times.

—Dean Smith

Have you ever owned a car that you deeply regretted buying every single mile you drove it? Owning a bad car is like getting struck with the stomach flu for a hundred thousand miles. You feel horrible every single moment, and the money runs out of your wallet like water from a faucet.

In the moments before I purchased the worst mistake of my life, there was a little voice that urged me to look around for a few more days. But I overrode that voice with my own wisdom.

Within the first thirty days, we'd paid $700 for a new fuel pump. Then there was a smattering of little repairs here and little repairs there. A year later, the engine began making a weird noise. Weird noises in our cars are like the train's whistle to let you know that something big is coming and you're about to get flattened.

When our car was in the shop and all of our kids were in after-school activities, I felt like I was having ten panic attacks a day. For weeks my husband and I juggled our lives with one working car. Yes, I know that there are families who live happy lives with one vehicle, and now we can too. But back then, we couldn't, and I thought I'd lose my mind.

Two weeks later, the repair shop called. I don't even know what was wrong with the car. I paid the bill with money that we didn't have to spare and drove off into the sunset.

A few weeks later, our minivan stopped running.

If you've ever owned a car that the devil himself would never drive, you totally know how I feel right now. Every time you hear a noise or clunk, a worried little voice whispers, *Not again!* That morning I sat in the driver's seat, repeatedly turning the key in the ignition and willing my car to start. An apple-size pit banged around in my stomach making me sick because I knew I couldn't handle whatever was wrong. My hands shook as I called the repair shop. *Surely they would agree to look at the car without charge since they'd just repaired it.*

The mechanic called a week later to tell me that our minivan from H-E-Double Hockey Sticks needed a replacement engine. What happened next isn't difficult for you to visualize: imagine a tall, black woman wearing a ponytail, pop-bottle glasses, a too-big T-shirt, and ill-fitting capris. Now imagine her dropping onto her kitchen floor, wailing.

I experienced the adult version of what parents of toddlers like to call a *meltdown*. In short, a meltdown is an uncontrolled expression of hopelessness. Meltdowns mean that you've run out of mental and emotional resources to deal with your uncertainty and worry. If meltdown had a slogan, I wouldn't be able to print it because my mom would have to wash my mouth out with soap.

Yes, there are worse things going on in our world than a cracked engine block, but in that moment, I felt like my world was coming to an end. All of a sudden, I could totally relate to my kids when they lost their little minds in the grocery store over not getting the cereal with the pretty colored marshmallows.

As I lay on the floor, sobbing, my head began to throb. My body felt sapped of all energy. The weight of the world pressed down upon my body, and I just couldn't move. Even if I tried to move, my arms and legs were so tight that it actually hurt. Did you know that emotional and mental meltdowns cause actual physical pain? Our anxiety, worry, or extreme mental stress causes our body to experience pain, and our mental stress is often the culprit behind chronic pain symptoms.[1] So, as I lay on the floor, apocalyptic thoughts ran through my mind, slamming into one side of my brain after another.

> *We don't have the money for this!*
> *We're never going to get out of this.*
> *We're doomed!*

I'm guessing you can relate to my meltdown. Let me just clear something up: I've had other meltdowns over extreme stress or worry. During one other memorable meltdown, I lost control and threw a plate into a window. I'm not proud of that moment. But I want you to know that if stress or worry has ever caused you to do or say stupid things, you aren't alone.

I'm excited to tell you about what happened next when Joshua had a meltdown. The place of hope that we're going to discover has nothing to do with Joshua's actions; rather, God restored Joshua in the midst of mental and emotional distress, and we can learn from his story and apply it to our lives.

Joshua's Meltdown

One of the reasons I admire Joshua is because he seemed to be a man who had it all together. The Bible records story after story of Joshua as a valiant warrior, rock star assistant, faithful follower, and now, brave leader of the Israelites.

But those aren't the reasons I like Joshua. I like him because he was a man just like us. He wasn't perfect, and as we're about to see, sometimes Joshua cut corners on God's instructions and had to deal with the consequences.

After winning the battle of Jericho, the Israelites were ecstatic. They followed God's unique battle plan, watched the giant wall of Jericho fall down, and carried out God's instructions for burning the city.

As the soldiers come back to camp, I can see our Israelite sister preparing a meal for the celebration supper that evening. The rest of the camp listened while the soldiers told them about what it was like to be up close and personal when the walls fell down. (If I had been there, I'd have asked how many steps it took to walk around Jericho seven times. I really love tracking steps on my Fitbit.)

While the people celebrated, Joshua began calculating again in preparation for their next target, the city of Ai. As he'd done before the Jericho conquest, Joshua sent two spies to check out this city located farther west. When the spies returned, they told Joshua that Ai wasn't heavily populated and not to worry about sending all of the soldiers. In fact, they said that only a few thousand soldiers would be needed, and the rest of the fighting men could stay home.

Joshua followed the spies' recommendations and only sent a few thousand soldiers, who set out to attack the city of Ai. This all seems well and good, except for one thing: Joshua never consulted God on whether or not to follow the spies' recommendations. Remember how God always provided Joshua with a plan in advance and then Joshua would confirm with God about the plan before acting? Well, not this time. And what Joshua didn't know was that someone in his camp had broken one of God's decrees, and that transgression would impact the entire camp.

What did Joshua do that we should avoid? He failed to consult with God before he acted. (Remember *Let God lead*?) This is something I've done more often than I want to admit.

It only takes two verses to capture what happened when the Israelites went to battle the soldiers at Ai: "So approximately 3,000 warriors were sent, but they were soundly defeated. The men of Ai chased the Israelites from the town gate as far as the quarries, and they killed about thirty-six who were retreating down the slope. The Israelites were paralyzed with fear at this turn of events, and their courage melted away" (Joshua 7:4-5).

Not only did the Israelites suffer defeat, but three dozen men were killed. All of a sudden, they began to falter in their confidence for the future. Notice how the end of the verse says that their courage melted away. It became like water. Leaving a chocolate bar in a car on a hot day comes to mind when I think about melting. There's nothing sadder than opening up a chocolate wrapper and dealing with runny chocolate dripping everywhere.

When Joshua heard of their defeat, he had a meltdown worthy of any toddler's respect. Along with the other leaders, Joshua tore his clothes and threw dust on his head. (During those times, throwing dust on oneself was a sign of grief.[2] Remember the phrase that you might have heard at a funeral: *ashes to ashes, dust to dust*).

Have you ever questioned God when you had a meltdown and were stuck in a pit of despair? People don't like to admit that they question God, but it's okay to admit it. In fact, Joshua started his lament to God with a page from the old generation of Israelites, who often complained in the desert that they would have been better off in Egypt. Joshua wailed out to God, "Oh, Sovereign Lord, why did you bring us across the Jordan River if you are going to let the Amorites kill us?" (Joshua 7:7).

Joshua expressed a feeling that we've all experienced when everything seems to be hopeless. We want to go back to the good ol' days, to the way things used to be, even when the good ol' days weren't necessarily that good.

Joshua continued to pour his heart out and asked God a question: "For when the Canaanites and all the other people living in the land hear about it, they will surround us and wipe our name off the face of the earth. And then what will happen to the honor of your great name?" (Joshua 7:9).

In other words, Joshua was saying: *God, You promised our ancestors long ago that You'd give Your children this land. Then You told us that when we crossed the Jordan River you'd give us every square inch of this land. You parted the river for us to walk across on dry ground. So, what's going on, God? What's going on here? If You don't come through on Your promises, people won't know how great You truly are.*

Long before Joshua challenged God with this line of reasoning, Moses had also used this approach on more than one occasion to save the misbehaving Israelites from God's punishment. (See Exodus 32:1-14; Numbers 14:10-12.) Both times Moses prayed and reminded God that the Israelites' enemies were watching to see if God would keep His promises to preserve and protect His special possession. God relented from destroying the Israelites, but He did punish them.

At the core of the Israelites' defeat at Ai was the sin of a man named Achan, which affected the entire Israelite community. We'll talk about Achan in the next chapter, but for now, understand that God allowed Ai's army to defeat the Israelites to get their attention: something was wrong in their covenant community. But we'll see that God doesn't forget about His promises. Even as the Israelites were thrust into a difficult place, God would make sure that His glory was seen by the Canaanite kings throughout the land.

After Joshua's prayer, God gave a two-word command that stirs my soul when I read it. I've heard God speak these words into my own life when I've fallen down and fallen out. God said to Joshua, "Get up!" (Joshua 7:10).

When we have a meltdown, we're a lot like toddlers. We want to lie there like a sad lump. Not only are we in anguish, but we don't mind having an audience to see our misery as well.

The longer we're on the ground after a meltdown, the more we are in danger of believing that we're doomed. It's here that people start to explain their lives through the filter of a communication style that psychologist Martin Seligman calls the 3Ps: personalization, pervasiveness, and permanence.[3] When we're having a meltdown in a stressful situation it's easy for us to get stuck in our hopeless thinking like:

> *I'll never be able to figure this out.* (personalization)
> *My whole life sucks.* (pervasiveness)
> *Nothing is ever going to change.* (permanence)

If we play these tapes in our mind enough, our brains will stop looking for solutions, and we really might come to believe those statements to be true. If you've ever had thoughts like these, let me tell you in the most loving way that this is dangerous living for you, and I'd like for you to challenge those thoughts because they aren't true. Whenever we begin to feel hopeless in our situation, what we need is Someone stronger than us to help us get back on our feet. We can't do it alone!

Getting Back Up Again

Many years ago, someone told me that when I have a nightmare or when I'm overwhelmed with worry, I should ask myself, "Where was Jesus during my nightmare?" That question always sobers me because the truth is that in my worst worry moments, I usually only see myself suffering, but I never see God working in me or around me.

When it comes to getting back up after a meltdown, our first move is to invite God into our bad moment and ask Him to lift us out of our pit of despair.

In Psalm 40:1, King David reflected on a time when he was in a pit of despair. He doesn't tell us what happened that put him in the pit; we just know that he was in there. Of course, if you've ever been in the pit, the background story doesn't really matter because a pit is its own self-contained misery. Yet, in his worst moment, the first thing David anticipated was God's help. "I waited patiently for the Lord to help me, and he turned toward me and heard my cry."

What I love about that verse is that David knew that God would help, but God showed up and did so much more than that. He heard David's distress. God didn't show up in a huff and say, "Well, what have you done now?" Rather, He showed up in David's life with compassion. How many of us beat ourselves up before, during, and after our meltdown and then expect that God's going to treat us the same way. But He doesn't!

King David wrote that not only did God lift him out of the stinking and suffocating pit of despair, but He set David back in a place where he wouldn't fall in again and stood by him while he got himself back together. Don't we all want a friend who can pull us to safety and then stay with us while we get our bearings again? That's exactly what God promises to do for you when you're in a pit of despair.

Knowing that God can lift us up after we've melted down brings us such hope! I don't know about you, but I also want to know what I can do to keep from falling in such a pit again.

After God told Joshua to "get up," He explained the core reason behind the Israelites' defeat: sin. To get back on track, Joshua and the people had to discover the source of the sin and deal with it.

There is nothing sinful about having a meltdown. We all lose it sometimes. However, a meltdown is a symbol that we've tried and failed to do life apart from God's leading. Do you know that "pride" stands for *Please remember I do everything*? That one hurt, didn't it? Maybe it's just me.

For many years, my massive meltdowns occurred about twice

a year, when my nonstop schedule collided with either a health or a financial crisis (or both). Once all of my emotional or spiritual resources were depleted, I'd have to come to God in my distress, and like Joshua, I needed God to tell me to *get up*.

At that point, I'd take a few days off to step back and ask myself the hard questions about how I'd set myself up for that meltdown. Romans 2:4 illustrates how loving God is when we're running in the wrong direction in life: "Don't you see how wonderfully kind, tolerant, and patient God is with you? Does this mean nothing to you? Can't you see that his kindness is intended to turn you from your sin?"

> Sometimes a meltdown is a blessing because it gets our attention and reminds us to run back to God.

Sometimes a meltdown is a blessing because it gets our attention and reminds us to run back to God.

In order to prepare themselves to discover the source of sin, the Israelites had to stop and reflect on their lives and examine themselves to see what they might be thinking or doing that would be sinful and need to be confessed. The Scriptures use the word "consecrate" to explain this process.

Socrates is credited with saying, "An unexamined life is not worth living." When we aren't willing to look at ourselves, meaning our attitudes, actions, or character, then we're bound to miss out or mess up. In our fast-paced society, we're bombarded with all kinds of ideas and gadgets, as well as new ways of thinking. How can we know if we're sliding off track if we don't stop for a scriptural temperature check from time to time?

When's the last time you stopped to think about how you were living? Most people don't realize that the Sabbath should be a vital weekly opportunity to stop and just sit in our humanity. Most often, we're not comfortable with thinking about how we're doing because we're so quick to judge or justify our actions. Yet, deep inside, we hate the tension that Paul identified in Romans 7:15: "I don't really understand myself, for I want to do what is right, but I don't do it. Instead I do what I hate."

What if you could prevent a future meltdown by identifying the places in your heart where you're trying to do life without God? Are you willing to invite God to help you do a spiritual temperature check? It's a good idea to do a spiritual temperature check if you'd rate your level of stress at a seven out of ten, or if the busyness of your life has kept you from church or your small group for more than four weeks in a row. A spiritual temperature check is a good idea if you've felt unmotivated to pray or do your Bible study. The temperature check isn't a pass/fail exercise, but rather a technique to help you reverse direction away from a meltdown, which we'd all like to avoid.

One of the psalmists provided a guide for your spiritual temperature check that is so helpful for our battle against worry. "Search me, O God and know my heart; test me and know my anxious thoughts" (Psalm 139:23). If you follow that psalmist's prayer, you can do a spiritual temperature check. It might be helpful to have a notebook handy if you do this.

Step 1 is to invite God into every area of your life. He's always present and knows everything about you, but now you are acknowledging that instead of living like God isn't paying attention to you. If you need words to say, you can use these:

> Dear God, I give You permission to invade every thought, every action, and every attitude that I've had over the past few months. I don't remember everything, but You do. God, where are the places of anxiety and worry in my life?

God, remind me of the times when I left You out of my decision-making or my actions.

God, show me the times when I treated others unkindly or without compassion.

God, what are the activities that distract me from following You?

God, are there any people, places, or things that I need to remove from my life because they are harming me?

God, where are the places of concealed sin in my heart?

God, what worries need to be eliminated from my life?

God, am I too busy?

God, can You show me how precious I am to You?

Step 2 is to just sit quietly with your notebook and wait for God to speak. This is hard! If this is your first time doing it, know that God won't use audible words, but you may begin to remember certain things. As you remember them, write them down. If you sense God telling you to do something, write that down too.

After you feel that you've written down enough, step 3 is to repent. Do you want to keep doing the things that keep you worried or anxious? Are there certain attitudes or behaviors that you need to abandon in order for you to grow closer to God? Whatever your next step, you can make that declaration to God as you close your time with Him. Again, if you need words, you can use these:

Dear God, thank You for giving me insight into where I am in my heart and mind. God, I don't want to think or behave in ways that keep me from following You. I want to turn away from

_____ .

Help me to turn toward You in every area of my life so that I can live free from worry and enjoy peace because of You. In Jesus's name, amen.

Getting up the courage to examine your life is an intentional step toward avoiding a meltdown. You can repeat this temperature check exercise whenever your internal pressure mounts or you sense a meltdown in your future.

One final thought:
Getting back up after a meltdown begins with asking God for help.

12

What If God Doesn't Give Me What I Want?

Whatever secrets you hide often create fear and worry inside.

—Barb Roose

*T*his is the story that I've dreaded telling because it highlights one of the times in life when fear and worry got the best of me.

It all began one evening as my family and I strolled around the block for our routine after-dinner walk. We live in a historical neighborhood filled with nineteenth- and twentieth-century homes that involve the three R's of any older home: *remodel, restore, repeat.*

As we walked, I noticed a new For Sale sign posted in the yard of a home near my house. At the time, it was a seller's market, so lots of homes were for sale, but this one caught my eye. My husband and I agreed to attend the open house the upcoming weekend.

When I stepped into the listed house a few days later, I felt at home. It's been almost two decades, and I still remember standing in the entry and looking left into the living room. Immediately, I saw my smiling family enjoying warm winter nights playing board games in front of the fireplace. To my right, I could picture our family celebrating holidays and birthdays in the dining room around our extended Neiman Marcus table with its five—yes, five—extension inserts. My heart dipped a little when we went into the kitchen and I saw the blue-gray carpet on the floor. For me, kitchen carpet is like owning a fabric toilet bowl. No matter how much you flush, it's never clean. I perked up as I imagined cooking in that space surrounded by new cabinets and hardwood floors.

For all of my vivid imaginations, my husband only saw the listing price plus the mortgage that we were paying on our existing home. He did agree that we could put our home on the market and see what would happen.

A short time later, the Realtor called. She wanted me to know that multiple offers were coming in on the house. Our home had just gone on the market, and we had no bites. So when she warned me that her listing would likely sell in the near future to the highest bidder, I panicked. After visualizing my family growing up in that home, I couldn't let that dream get away from me. So I did something that still galls me today. I bought that dream house without telling my husband.

Now, when I say "bought," what I mean is that I signed a full-price purchase contract for the new home. Even with that explanation, it still sounds bad. And you know what else was bad? When I told my husband about my shenanigans that night, it did not go well.

Have you ever heard that saying about how God watches out for babies and fools? Well, He does. God watched over me during my growing years and later as a straight-up fool who bought a house that could have put my marriage and family in financial jeopardy. My literal saving grace was an addendum in the sales agreement that my existing home had to sell first. That little addendum allowed me to wiggle myself off the hook and away from the deal.

God allowed me to follow my intense desire to show me the dangers of trying to grab what He wasn't ready to give to me. What God wants to give me, He brings to me, either in opportunities to pursue or as a gift He drops in my lap. I've learned to be wary of anything that I'm tempted to cut corners to try to get.

Oh, Be Careful Little Eyes What You See

In the last chapter, you read about how Joshua and the Israelites suffered a meltdown after their defeat at Ai. While Joshua neglected to consult God for a final battle plan and the Israelites let their pride get in the way, the real reason for their defeat was because of one man's sin that sabotaged the entire Israelite community.

After God told Joshua to get up, He told the Israelites to consecrate themselves because He would show up the next morning and reveal the guilty party. The covenant agreement that bound them together in community stood for one for all and all for the One. This is why one person's sin would affect the entire community. Yet, God offered time for the offending party to come forward before the next morning and foretold his or her punishment. No one spoke up.

So, the next day, God conducted multiple elimination rounds, beginning with the tribe of Judah, down through Judah's tribal clans, then through the groups of families, drilled down to specific families, before a man named Achan was called forward.

Have you ever had that moment when you knew you were about to be found out? Perhaps you stole something or lied. King David eloquently captured how awful we feel when we've sinned but refuse to confess. After his affair with a married woman and the murder of her husband, King David wrote, "When I refused to confess my sin, my body wasted away, and I groaned all day long" (Psalm 32:3). When we sit on our sin, it makes us sick because the guilt and worry wear on our bodies, spirits, and souls.

Joshua implored Achan to come clean and began with, "My son, give glory to the Lord, the God of Israel by telling the truth" (Joshua

7:19). Confession is a powerful action of worship because it calls us to crush our pride and admit our wrongdoing to God. Joshua's words are also to be admired. He demonstrated such gentleness in speaking to Achan, who knew that he was in deep weeds without bug spray. He'd just seen his men routed by the Ai army, and thirty-six of those men were killed. Yet, instead of screaming at Achan or berating him for being the cause of their misfortune, Joshua maintained an attitude that we can learn from. When something goes wrong and someone else is to blame, we must value our relationship over being right. You can see Joshua doing this by reminding Achan that he is still part of the covenant community and part of God's special family. Joshua didn't attack Achan; rather, he calmly addressed him.

Then Achan confessed. Even though God had commanded the Israelite soldiers not to take anything from the ruins at Jericho, Achan took some items anyway. Notice the words that follow every time that Achan used the pronoun *I*: "Among the plunder, *I saw* a beautiful robe from Babylon, 200 silvers coins, and a bar of gold weighing more than a pound. *I wanted* them so much that *I took* them" (Joshua 7:21, emphasis added).

Have you ever seen something or someone that you wanted so badly that you created good, rational reasons why it was okay to disobey God? *I know that this isn't right, but I know that God will forgive me....I know that this relationship doesn't honor God, but we're really in love....I think that God was planning to give this to me anyway, so I might as well get it now.*

To be clear, what Achan stole was no small thing. The value of the robe, silver, and gold was equivalent to a year's wage.[1] Still, the monetary value of Achan's theft paled in comparison to the spiritual impact of his sin on the Israelite community. Not only did they suffer death and demoralizing defeat, but Achan's inner motives reveal a shocking and scary insight that was true not only for him but for the entire community—and all of us: We can see God moving around us, but unless we allow God to move within us, we will be unmoved.

How could Achan walk across the dry Jordan River and watch God collapse the walls of Jericho and still disobey? Perhaps the same reason why I could do my Bible study one morning and turn around and buy a house without telling my husband that night.

> We can see God moving around us, but unless we allow God to move within us, we will be unmoved.

Sin never seems like sin, only a simple, harmless moment. First, Achan saw. *Look at all of the stuff lying around. Check out that robe. I'd look great in that! No one in Jericho will miss it because they're all dead.* The word "saw" is the same Hebrew word *raah* used in Genesis 3 when describing how Eve *saw* the fruit on the tree. That situation didn't end well either. A few of the definitions of *raah* are "keep on looking" or "make an inspection."[2] Whenever I keep desserts in my house, I tend to "see" them a lot. The longer I look at those sugary sweets, the more I want them. I've actually had to stop buying treats so I don't go searching for them.

In Achan's case, it wasn't the first look that got him into trouble; it was the second, longer look that prompted Achan to begin wanting those items that God had commanded the Israelites to leave alone.

Another word for "wanting" is "coveting." We don't use the word *covet* much, but if you had grown up in biblical times, it might sound familiar. One commentary describes the verb *covet* as "thoughts of the heart."[3]

You cannot see someone covet because it's an action hidden deep within. You'll never know if I covet your house, car, or shoe collection.

(Okay, the last one probably isn't true. If we happen to wear the same size, I'll make it clear that I really want your shoes.) The same commentator observed that ancient moralists believed that unless there was an offending action, then all thoughts and motives were free from scrutiny or need to control.[4] However, Proverbs 4:23 instructs us to be careful about what we allow ourselves to get attached to, especially when those people or things can drive a wedge between God and us: "Guard your heart above all else, / for it determines the course of your life."

When our hearts and minds entertain thoughts of actions that draw us away from God, it's only a matter of time before those actions actually happen.

Can you see Achan looking around, waiting for an opportune moment, when no one was looking, to snatch up the robe and the gold bar? As the other soldiers were checking to make sure they'd completed God's mission, Achan was completing his sin.

Once Achan grabbed the forbidden items, he had to hide them. If you've ever tried to hide anything, you know that the mental exhaustion that comes with keeping something secret is horrible. Achan might have stolen the items so that he could enjoy the payoff in the future, but he quickly discovered that his sin cost precious peace in the present.

I wonder: was it a hardened heart that prevented him from speaking up, or was it fear? In either event, Achan stayed silent, but everyone found out his sin.

In the difficult scene that followed, the Israelites ran to Achan's tent and confirmed his story by retrieving the forbidden items. Next, the entire Israelite community went down to the Valley of Achor with Achan, his entire household, and all of his belongings. As a punishment, Achan and his entire family were stoned. After the stoning, the area was burned. This is one of those difficult events in Scripture because we don't understand why God would command such a severe punishment.

You may wonder why God, if He is loving, would inflict such a harsh judgment. Perhaps you question other troublesome passages in the Old Testament, wondering if God is somehow different in the Old and New Testaments. In his book *When Did God Become a Christian?* author and pastor David Kalas explores this common struggle, showing that God's holiness and love are both clearly on display throughout the Scriptures, even in difficult passages. Drawing on the writings of Theodoret, a fifth-century monk and bishop from Syria, Kalas points out that sometimes we must look for the truth of God's heart—His desire to love and protect us—hidden within a Bible story or passage. He writes,

> Theodoret makes a logical connection between God's threats and God's love: "The reason that the God of all threatens punishment, you see, is not to inflict it on those he threatens but to strike them with fear and lead them to repentance, and by ridding them of their wicked behavior extend to them salvation. After all, if he wanted to punish, he would not threaten punishment; instead, by threatening he makes clear that he longs to save and not to punish."[5]

We see throughout the Scriptures that God wants to save His people from sin—something He ultimately accomplishes through the death of His own Son. Yet as Melissa Spoelstra points out in her study on the Book of Numbers, there are some distinctions in the way that God interacts with His people in the Old and New Testaments, who were living under two different covenants. She offers these helpful insights:

> We see differences in the people, circumstances, and methods of interaction between God and His creation [in the Old and New Testaments]. What we do *not* see ... are any differences in the *character* of God. Throughout the Scriptures, God Himself is unchanging.... God is both just and gracious in His interactions with His people living under each covenant.... One commentator put it this

way, 'Defiant sin is the spiritual equivalent of jumping off the Golden Gate Bridge. If biblical warnings sound harsh, they are to prevent that from happening.' Like a loving parent who sets boundaries and rules, our loving God wants what is best for us. God wants to protect us, and He knows all too well that sin is never safe.[6]

As a Christ-follower, I've learned that God's holiness will always make me uncomfortable. We cannot comprehend God's holiness and the extent to which sin offends His presence, but we must be aware of it.

Achan's story makes us feel uncomfortable because we feel that one bad action shouldn't result in complete annihilation. Yet, that perspective reveals that we do not see sin from God's vantage point. Romans 6:23 tells us that the wages (or consequences) of sin is death, whether that sin arises from what we think, what we say, or what we do. We don't like Achan's story because of his violent physical death, yet sin can cause death to our relationships, health, spiritual growth, finances, and marriages. This is why God hates sin; He knows it will strangle us.

One Word Gives a Way Out

One of the sobering lessons from my house-buying mistake is that my worry and panic caused me to act in a way that put my family at risk. I was worried that God wouldn't give me what I want, so I grabbed for it without regard to the cost to us all.

It's easy to look down on Achan for his sin, but we've all shared his greedy heart. How many of us have seen things that we wanted and taken them even though they weren't God's best for us? Even if we didn't steal the items, we bought what we couldn't afford, what we didn't need, or what ended up distracting us from God.

Maybe you haven't stolen something, like Achan, but how often do you worry that God won't give you what you want? Perhaps you worry that God will give you something different from what you see for your life.

What if God wants something different for my singleness?
What if God wants something different for my career?
What if God wants something different for my fertility?
What if God wants something different for my health?
What if God wants something different for my children?
What if God wants something different for my marriage?

I'm not sure which one of those questions is a trigger for you, but when we're afraid that God won't give us what we want, we might be tempted to grab for it another way. Like Abram and Sarai, who wanted a child but didn't want to wait for God's timing. Instead, they came up with their own solution and created a lot more heartache for themselves, Hagar, and young Ishmael (see Genesis 16, 21). Their fears over "me" ended up in disaster for the entire "we" of their family.

Confess to God to Free Yourself

In her teens, Tam Hodge underwent not one, but two abortions. A few years later, she went to church with a friend and met her future husband, Brent. Not long after that, Tam accepted Christ. But her secret remained a secret, even after getting married.

In her book, *And Now I Choose*, Tam shares the story of the dark days after her daughter, Kass's, birth. She lived with constant guilt over her past abortions, and just a few days after her daughter's birth, Tam sank into a deep depression. "I knew I was depressed. And I knew the 'why' behind it, but I couldn't tell [Brent] the true why yet.... I believed that God was going to take her to punish me."[7]

As her depression raged, Tam begged God to let her sweep her past under the rug so that she could protect her secret. She wanted to keep the peace, but God kept whispering to her, *There is no peace.* Tam goes on to say, "He showed me how tormented I was inside as memories, lies and times of hiding began racing through my mind. I was preoccupied with the fear of my secret getting out."[8]

You don't have to have had an abortion to see yourself in Tam's story. Any sin that you try to cover up will begin to eat you up. As they say, you are only as sick as your secrets.

When her baby was five months old, Tam had had enough. She cried out to God that she was done keeping her secret. Then, something happened: "That's when I realized that I had just arrived at the end of Tam's road. Now it was time to merge onto God's road."[9]

Tam gave glory to God when she stopped trying to hold on to her secret and chose to cling to her Savior. It was then that she found freedom and God provided a way forward for her to live free from guilt and shame. John 8:32 says, "The truth will set you free." Secrets pretend to shield us, but they actually hold us down in shame and condemnation. Secrets strangle us. Then we end up suffocating our relationships because we're constantly waiting for Chicken Little's sky to fall down on our lives.

The next morning, after Tam had confessed to God and Brent, she woke up feeling different. "I started to feel like a brand-new person. Healing and freedom began to take up residence in me."[10] It was then that Tam began to tell her friends, and within a few years, she wrote her book and began speaking to audiences around the country. I'm so blessed because she is one of my friends!

What's the word of the day? Confession. That's the action step for this chapter. Is it time to say the words?

Do you realize that God gave Achan a chance to confess? I don't know if that would have changed his punishment, but Achan was given a chance to come forward and confess his guilt. If they knew, Achan's family members were given a chance to confess what they knew. But they didn't either.

If you're reading this today and you find yourself in a similar position as Achan, God's mercy is realized for you in this moment as well. Breathe in the hope and wisdom of Proverbs 28:13: "People who conceal their sins will not prosper, but if they confess and turn from them, they will receive mercy."

You've been given this moment of mercy right now. Take it, my friend. Give glory to God by confessing what you've done. Right now you have a chance to speak up and make things right. Do you need to return something so that you can sleep peacefully at night? Do you need to confess to something so that you can stop being afraid of getting found out? If you aren't sure who to call, contact your pastor, Bible study teacher, or small group leader. If you don't have a pastor or your pastor isn't available, call a local Christian radio station, like K-Love (see klove.com), and they will direct you to the right person.

Yes, depending on your situation, there may be consequences, but you're already living with the painful consequences of persistent guilt and shame. The consequences of telling the truth will be much easier to bear than suffocating under a thousand-pound brick of worry, guilt, and shame.

Whatever it is, God's giving you an opportunity to do the right thing!

13

Are You a Worrier
or a Warrior?

There is a great difference between worry and concern. A worried person sees a problem and a concerned person solves a problem.

—Harold Stephens

As a kid, I loved watching *Wonder Woman* on network television. Back in the day, Wonder Woman's alter ego, Diana Prince, wore owl-eyed glasses and sensible suits. When trouble called, all it took was a few twirls and some smoky camouflage for suitable Diana to be replaced by a glamazon superhero with perfect vision, fabulous hair, and a golden lasso. As a little girl who wore giant pop-bottle glasses, I wanted to twirl around and have my glasses disappear too. That never happened, but my mom paid to make my glasses disappear in tenth grade when I finally got contacts.

Over the past decade, Hollywood has jumped on the *woman as warrior* bandwagon. During one of the most powerful scenes in the *Wonder Woman* movie reboot, Wonder Woman ventures to cross no man's land during World War I to save a community under siege. As she leaves the safety of the bunker, her friends yell for her to stop so that she doesn't get killed. It doesn't take long for the enemy to begin firing at the lone woman crossing the field. Wonder Woman deflects their bullets with her arm guards and shields. Then the enemy soldiers begin unloading their automatic weapons and heavy artillery. As Wonder Woman bears down under the fiery assault, the men she had left behind race to join her. Inspired by her bravery, they charge the field, and together they overtake the enemy's bunker. For me, it's easy to see Wonder Woman charging a field, taking on bad guys and saving the day. She's got superpowers, a golden lasso, strong abs, and great hair. But what about the rest of us? What if we don't feel like Wonder Woman? What if we feel more like Worry Woman instead?

Does the *woman as warrior* theme translate to regular women like you and me? Yes! While genteel women of the past might have gotten offended, I think that there is a fighter in all of us. There were women like Mary Ludwig Hayes, who fought with her husband during the American Revolutionary War in the 1700s. When he went to fight, she jumped in to serve too. Mary is remembered by her nickname Molly Pitcher because she supplied tired soldiers and wounded men with water during the fighting. One soldier wrote in his diary about how Mary fired cannons alongside her husband during battle. In one entry he recorded that when the enemy's cannon shot passed between Mary's legs, destroying the bottom of her petticoat, she glanced down at her petticoat and, without showing much concern, continued fighting. Over the years, Mary's nickname became the female complement to the male moniker G.I. Joe.[1]

Think about the stories of how the generations of women in your family fought to keep their family together. These women fought for survival when crops failed, jobs were lost, husbands died, or children got sick. I think about unsung historical heroes, like slave women, a pioneer wife, or a Civil War widow. Like some of us, those women were on the front lines of some of America's greatest challenges, holding together homes and families during uncertain times and dangerous conditions.

As women, we face so many different places of battle. I'd like to think that there's a little Molly Pitcher in all of us. To deal with what we're up against these days with family challenges, social issues, and world instability, we need to be like Molly Pitcher. Our primary trouble spot is located in the space between our ears. It's in this space where we decide if we will be a worrier or a warrior.

All of us are fighting for something, but worriers fight one way and warriors fight another. Worriers fight themselves while warriors fight the problem. Worriers feel isolated in their struggle while warriors know that they can't win without a team. Forgive me for saying this, but worriers have a loser mentality. They worry about what will be lost, so they hunker down in fear. Warriors fight to win because they have something worth fighting for. If they lose, worriers feel vindicated because they expected to lose. If a warrior loses, they aren't deterred. Warriors regroup and go out to fight again. Lisa Bevere, author of *Girls with Swords*, quotes British prime minister Margaret Thatcher's famous words, "You may have to fight a battle more than once to win it."[2]

We all want to be warriors. If that's your pick, it's time to learn how warriors fight to win. It's time to learn how to *fight in faith*, which is what happens when we put our fighting friends to work under the power of the Holy Spirit.

Fighting in faith is a visual representation of what it looks like to face hardship, difficulty, or uncertainty like a warrior instead of fighting in fear like a worrier. We've got to see ourselves on the battlefield standing strong. But what does that look like? Fighting in faith paints a picture of you standing tall with peace, courage, and strength standing with you. It gets you into position for God's power to give you victory over whatever worry is trying to wear you out.

Fighting in faith is different from spiritual warfare. Fighting in faith is about how we fight, while spiritual warfare is about who and what we are fighting. The Scriptures tell us that in this world, we're fighting against unseen, dark powers led by Satan to derail our pursuit of God and destroy us mentally, physically, and relationally. That is spiritual warfare, but fighting in faith is our strategy for spiritual warfare. Your fighting friends can be used in any spiritual warfare situation, and they will get you into position for God's victory every time.

Getting Back OUT There

When we experience failure, getting back up again is tough. That's where Joshua and the Israelites were after their loss at the battle of Ai and the violent punishment of one of their own who'd sinned.

Immediately after their lowest moment since entering the Promised Land, God redirected Joshua's attention back to the plan to conquer the land. God didn't let them wallow. He got them right back into action. God's directives to Joshua began with, "Don't be afraid or discouraged." Aren't those the words you want someone to say to you after a major mess-up? After something bad happens, God wants us to get back in the fight again. He doesn't want you afraid of the battle because the battle belongs to Him.

Joshua knew his men didn't have the same kinds of weapons, horses, or chariots as their enemies. But God never planned on the Israelites having those battle enhancements. Nothing wrong with those weapons, but God wanted the Israelites to know that, even if they fought, He was the One to bring victory. The Israelites were no match for their enemies. As Proverbs 21:31 says, "The horse is prepared for the day of battle, but victory belongs to the Lord."

Are there times when you don't think you have what it takes to win? Have you ever considered that God intentionally leaves a gap between what you have and what you need so He can fill that space? When we have what we need to handle our problems, one of the potential side effects is that we think we don't need God, otherwise known as pride.

In 1 Kings, the king of Aram, Ben-hadad, mobilized his army to attack Samaria, the capital city of Israel at the time. He sent a note to Israel's evil King Ahab demanding Ahab's treasure and his family. Ahab complied, yet Ben-hadad sent more demands. This time, Ahab's advisers told him not to give in to any more demands. After Ahab denied Ben-hadad's request, the king of Aram was incensed and proclaimed that he would annihilate Samaria. Ahab answered with this wisdom: "A warrior putting on his sword for battle should not boast like a warrior who has already won" (1 Kings 20:11).

You might be really smart and resourceful or you might have enough money and connections. Whatever you've got on your side is helpful, but like horses and chariots, whatever you've got still doesn't guarantee you a victory that is lasting and secure. If you've got a child who is fighting a substance addiction, you can have access to the best rehab centers, doctors, self-help books, and insurance, but you still don't have control over that child's addiction or his or her will. If your marriage is struggling and you're worried about your spouse leaving, you can go to marriage conferences, meet with your pastor, and track his phone, but that's no guarantee that you can save your relationship.

There's nothing wrong with marshaling all your resources, but don't fool yourself into thinking that your skills or smarts are the same price as God's divine security. Instead, offer what you have to God and let Him use it according to His plan and purpose.

After telling Joshua not to be discouraged or afraid, God affirmed His promise to Joshua that He would deliver victory for the Israelites. God promised to give Joshua the king of Ai, his people, his town, and his land. Here we learn the first principle of fighting in faith: *you must claim God's promise.* God told Joshua that He would give them the land, and Joshua believed it.

How precious would it have been for Joshua to hear God say, "Even though all y'all messed up, I'm still giving you what I promised you"? It's like the Christmas when I discovered that one of my kids had unwrapped a few gifts under the tree. I was so mad that I packed up the gifts and put them away for a few days. However, I still pulled out the gifts and gave them with complete joy on Christmas morning. When the Israelites, hundreds of years later, were at their lowest because of their disobedience, God repeated a promise that echoed His words to Joshua: "Don't be afraid, for I am with you. Don't be discouraged, for I am your God. I will strengthen you and help you. I will hold you up with my victorious right hand" (Isaiah 41:10). I don't know if you know this, but the right hand is symbolic of blessing and strength. Even at our worst, God's promises are true for us, even if we've derailed ourselves in that moment. God's promises are always possible for you and me.

After offering encouragement and confirming His promise, God told Joshua to take all of the fighting men to fight Ai. Since the memory of their defeat was still fresh in their minds, it would have taken courage to go back out to fight again. The second principle of fighting in faith is that *there is courage in numbers*. It's tough be to courageous when you feel alone, but the Israelites had their entire team and God on their side. All of the soldiers showed up to begin executing God's unique strategy. At Jericho, the men marched in silence for seven days before shouting. This time, Joshua divided the soldiers and sent them to positions in different locations near the town of Ai, including an ambush behind the town.

In a bold move, Joshua and the army marched in front of Ai on their way to setting up camp in the valley. When the king of Ai saw the Israelite soldiers, he hurried to send out his soldiers to attack. Part of the battle plan included the Israelite army feigning retreat. As Ai's soldiers chased the Israelites away from their town, it not only led them toward the Israelite ambush but also pulled them away from defending the town.

There's much to admire about Joshua's courage as he purposefully drew the attention of the Ai army. I don't know about you, but after I've fallen on my face, my gut reaction is to play it safe. If I've put myself out there and gotten crushed, the next time I only want to poke a toe out there first. However, Joshua went all in with God's plan and didn't hold back out of fear.

My husband loves to say, "If you're going to be a bear, be a grizzly." That's good advice. If we've got a challenge in our lives, we need to meet the challenge head-on and stop dancing around it. Do you have a financial crisis that tempts you to run in fear because you're afraid to find out how much debt you actually owe? Has the doctor told you to lose weight in order to better manage a health condition, but you keep making up excuses why you can't work out? Do you know that your marriage is struggling, but you don't say anything because you're afraid that your spouse will want a divorce? If you've got a threat to your life, get up in the face of it, in Jesus's name, and attack. Open the envelopes and add up the debt, call a friend to join the gym with you, or make the appointment to see the counselor and talk things through. Whatever your situation, it's worth fighting for!

Once the Israelites ambushed the enemy, Ai never had a chance. Not only did Joshua and the Israelites defeat the army, but they followed God's instructions and destroyed the town after they conquered it. This demonstrated the third principle of fighting in faith: *obedience builds spiritual strength.*

As a result of their belief in God's promises, their courage, and their obedience, everything that God promised came true for Joshua and the Israelites. They had complete victory over the king and his army; they conquered the town and its people and possessed the land.

Drill to Become an Awesome Warrior

Have you noticed how similarly the words *worrier* and *warrior* are spelled? Both begin with *w* and end with *r*, with a double *r* in the middle. Yet, what happens in between tells the real story.

When I think about the *a* in warrior, I associate it with the word *assertive*. A warrior runs to the fight, engages the enemy, and knows how to fight effectively. The key to assertiveness is preparation. Consequently, I associate the *o* in worrier with the word *obstacle*. Worriers only see problems in their own ability to deal with both the situation and the problems blocking their victory.

Practically speaking for our worry battle, worriers think and feel fear while warriors find helpful ways to express and act on concern. Author Harold Stephen says, "There is a great difference between worry and concern. A worried person sees a problem and a concerned person solves a problem."[3] A concerned person doesn't need permission to act assertively on a concern.

For several years, my friend Ellie wore her warrior boots. Her son lived in Mexico while she lived in the United States. After her marriage collapsed, Ellie came to the United States, but due to immigration issues, her son had to stay behind in an unstable and dangerous situation with his father. For years, Ellie fought to overcome sickening worry and focus on actionable concerns. She spent more than a hundred thousand dollars on attorneys, consultants, and travel to try to get custody. At times she'd take a break from the overwhelming stress to go on retreats. But then Ellie would regroup and move forward again. Twice, Ellie put her life in danger launching courageous missions with armed personnel to try to gain custody of her son. She kept praying, and eventually, a set of circumstances unfolded that allowed Ellie to make a large-sum settlement to her ex-husband in exchange for legal custody. She and her child are reunited, and Ellie knows that God gave her not only a tangible victory by allowing her child to come to America but also a spiritual victory as well.

Have you ever heard that quotation comparing worry to a rocking chair? Worry gives us the appearance of productivity, but it is so unproductive because the only thing that changes when we worry is our level of worry. Worry is like black mold growing in your mind. I hope that picture is gross enough to stick with you. Worry spreads and makes us sick, but we have another choice.

For every worry you face, is there a healthy concern you can act upon? If you're worried about your finances, is there a person you can call for advice? If you are worried about your health, is there an action plan that your doctor has given you to follow? If you are worried about your adult child's destructive behavior, have you read books on keeping healthy boundaries and protecting your assets? If you're worried about your spiritual journey, have you made an appointment with your pastor?

Once you wrap your mind around the idea that there are healthy ways to act on your concerns, then how do you set yourself up so that you express concern instead of worry in the future?

That's where the 4P drill comes in handy! If you want to be a warrior over a worrier, commit this drill to memory and practice it so that when you are tempted to churn in worry, you can actually shift over to acting in healthy ways that express your concern.

Repeat God's Promises. Just as God constantly repeated His promises to Joshua, you also need to repeat God's promises to yourself. Think about the five "starter train" passages that you learned in chapter 4.

Give Yourself the Gift of the Present. Since our fears and worries are attached to uncertainty over the future, the best way to short-circuit them after repeating God's promises over them is to shift your thinking from the future to the present. I repeat to myself, "Barb, focus on right here and right now. God will take care of the future." When I say those words, my mind leaves the land of uncertainty and I can focus on a productive next step in my present circumstance.

Pray. Worry is talking to yourself, while praying is talking to God. When I find myself falling into worry, I shift the conversation from me, myself, and I to inviting God into the dialogue. When I invite God into my conversation, it's hard for me to drone on and on about my pitiful life. Instead, a genuine conversation with God will always remind me that He is present in my circumstance and He will take care of me right now and in the future.

Provide. If there is someone in my life that I'm tempted to worry about, I don't have to obsess about all the ways her life is going down the drain. Instead, I can be a healthy blessing to her by making a ten-minute phone call, sending an uplifting card, making a meal for her family, or taking her out to coffee and just letting her share what she is going through. How much more could we love people by actually reaching out to them instead of worrying about them? They'd feel much better when they experience our love, and frankly, so would we.

This 4P drill captures four healthy ways for you to be assertive and show concern as an alternative to just spinning your wheels in worry. Try it!

One final thought:
When you know the difference between worry and concern, you can be a powerful example of God's love instead panicking over what you can't control.

❧ 14 ❧

Secondhand Worry

We have to let the people in our lives discover
their own need for God.

—Tim Butler

One Sunday afternoon I received a Facebook message from someone asking for help.

This sweet lady, whom I'll call Leah, lost her father recently. If you've lost a parent or any loved one, you know that grief runs deep. Dealing with the grief requires time, rest, and lots of self-care. Yet, Leah was unable to care for herself. You'll soon understand why.

Leah was overwhelmed—except the worries weren't her own. She was drowning in the worries of loved ones around her; they had pushed *their* cares onto her. I've known Leah almost my entire life. She manages her personal affairs well and plans for the future. Yet, she felt ensnared because of her fear, uncertainty, and worries about her adult children. One was experiencing a second, unplanned pregnancy and another had neglected to take care of some serious legal issues and was looking at jail time.

Leah told me that she had promised money, time, and energy to help her loved ones get through their situation. But she also admitted that this cycle of being stressed-out and bailing others out had been going on for years. In fact, before Leah's father passed away, he had gently warned Leah that taking on other people's problems would destroy her.

He was right.

I diagnosed Leah's condition as "secondhand worry."

You might be suffering from secondhand worry if someone tells you about his or her problems and you end up suffering physical and emotional symptoms. Another symptom of secondhand worry is when you are driven to assume responsibility for someone else's problem. (If you're familiar with recovery principles, secondhand worry is worry-driven enabling.)

Here are some practical examples:

- When your child neglects to finish his or her homework assignment and you try to talk their teacher into accepting the work late or giving out a pass.
- When you fear that your spouse might be fired for being late again and you call his or her boss to make an excuse or tell an outright lie.

The problem with secondhand worry is that we experience all of the symptoms associated with worry—sleepless nights, a stressed-out feeling, a lack of appetite or overeating, frayed nerves—and the situation isn't even about us.

If you can relate to Leah, it's a difficult place to be. Life is hard enough trying to fight in faith for our own victory over worry. It's not possible for us to fight someone else's battle too.

Helicopters and Bubble Wrap

There are two tools associated with secondhand worry: helicoptering and bubble wrapping. Both offer false security, but we use them anyway. Helicoptering is when we hover over someone to make sure he stays safe and on the straight and narrow according to our definition. Bubble wrapping happens when we actually limit or deny someone a life experience in order to keep him safe. In short, with helicoptering, we hover for fear that someone cannot make good decisions for his own life. With bubble wrapping, we won't even let him try. (That way we don't have to worry about him.)

For years, I felt like a Black Hawk helicopter mom because one of my kids has attention deficient hyperactivity disorder (or ADHD for short, because no one has the time to keep spelling out the entire disorder). I spent her toddler years tracking her like a NASA satellite because she moved like a danger-seeking missile. I purchased and unapologetically used an elastic wrist tether to attach us together after an awful Code Adam (lost child alert) at the grocery store. Testing in kindergarten revealed that my daughter met *all* of the criteria for ADHD. My husband and I agreed on our method of treatment, and we were able to better manage her symptoms.

But that didn't stop my helicopter parenting. I hovered over Samantha, monitoring her every move—from getting dressed in the morning to how and what she ate. It wasn't just vigilance; it was a worry-driven mentality that she couldn't thrive or survive without me.

In addition to helicoptering, bubble wrapping was also an issue for me. When my oldest daughter was admitted to West Point, we were thrilled at the honor and the opportunity for free tuition. However, as soon as we received her official admission letter, I began to worry about my daughter getting hurt and not being able to accept her appointment. In fact, when I joined the West Point Moms Facebook page, that's the first time I heard about bubble wrapping. Parents were canceling their students' plans to go skiing, motor-biking, or anything that could potentially cause an injury and interrupt their appointment to the military academy. My daughter didn't do any of those activities, but I spent a lot of time worrying about her getting into a bad car accident. During her final basketball season, she had a serious injury to her ankle. When I saw my tough girl rolling around on the floor, my first thought wasn't *Oh, no! She's injured!* My first thought was *Oh, no! What about West Point?!* That's horrible, right? But it was the truth. In fact, I got angry when her coach tried to reassure me that my daughter would be okay and not to worry. How dare she? Didn't she know that my daughter's future was at stake?

Helicoptering and bubble wrapping don't end when a person reaches adulthood. Furthermore, they aren't exclusive to parenthood. The adult version is called *micromanaging*. Bosses do it, but so do parents and grandparents of adults.

While I've told you all about my helicoptering and bubble wrapping, what I didn't tell you was how using those tools made me feel.

Tired.

So, so tired.

Constantly checking, hovering, hawking, calling, double-checking—all of it happening…all of the time. I could so relate to Jesus's words; my worries didn't add a moment to my girls' lives (see Matthew 6:27). In fact, all of my helicoptering shaved so many precious moments off of my life.

When I realized that my helicopter parenting and bubble-wrapping mentality was getting out of hand, I began seeing a Christian counselor. I knew I couldn't keep hovering over my kids out of fear. At the time, my counselor, Tim, and I had many heated discussions because I rebelled against his pointed questions about whether or not I was trying to play God in my children's lives. I told him he didn't understand that I was just trying to be a good mom and that good parents watch out for their kids. But Tim knew that my watching out included that "worst first" mentality that was making both me and my kids miserable. He challenged me with a question that I've carried and used many times with other helicopter parents: *Will you allow your children to discover their need for God?*

Uncomfortable Moments

After that experience, I realized that God did not put me on this planet to manage every one of my kids' choices. They were made for His purpose, and it was my job to point them to Him as much and as often as possible. So, I began to wrestle with these two questions:

1. Do I need to let my kids experience the natural consequences of their behaviors?
2. Will my actions undermine my kids' need for God?

Those two questions have been helpful guides for me as my kids moved through their teen and early adult years. Most of us discover our need for God once we run out of our own answers. I've been challenged, even as my kids were teens, to let them sit in uncomfortable moments. If they were getting a bad grade, performing poorly on a sports team, or lacking money for a desired item, these were all times I could help point them to God for help or guidance. While we can unconditionally love adults who repeatedly get fired, frequently overdraw their bank accounts, or abuse substances, we must create the space they need to be desperate for God. Have you considered that you might be the reason your prayers for their rescue haven't been answered?

Over the years, these two questions aided me in landing my helicopter. Still, my resolve was put to the test when one of my daughters came down with a common high school illness called "senioritis." It strikes most high school seniors with a serious symptom called I-don't-care-anymore. Two months before graduation, I received a letter from the school that began, "Mr. and Mrs. Roose, we must inform you that your daughter is in danger of not graduating from high school in May."

As parents, my husband and I had to step back and let our eighteen-year-old daughter learn as much from that experience as possible without calling her teachers and trying to smooth things over. We told her that we loved her, but that we could not take responsibility for her life. Together we brainstormed solutions as to how she could rectify the serious situation and let her know that we'd check in with her progress.

It was so hard to step back and let her be responsible for her life. But Samantha did amazingly well. She talked to her teachers, got her grades back on track, and graduated with her class. Best of all, she had the satisfaction of knowing that she took care of her responsibilities on her own.

How do we learn how to love others without taking responsibility for their worries? Later, we will discuss a tool that you and I can use to help us determine the all-important difference between getting caught in secondhand worry and expressing healthy forms of concern. But first we're going to look at what happened when Joshua and the Israelites got caught in a situation of secondhand worry. The consequences were long-lasting and far-reaching, so let's see what we can learn to avoid their mistake in our future.

Transfer of Worry

After the victory at Ai, the Israelites followed God's command to destroy the city. Afterward, Joshua circled up the Israelites, and they took time out to honor God. Joshua read God's Word to the people, including what they must do to be blessed, and what would bring curses into their lives. These were the same words that Moses had read to them before they entered the Promised Land. After a victory is a great time to refresh ourselves in God's words, because when things feel good and prosperous, our human nature leans away from God and toward extending our prosperity and good feelings.

As the Israelites celebrated God, the Canaanite kings were engaged in the equivalent of an angry group text thread. Considering how our world changed after 9/11, it's not hard to imagine that the kings might have discussed coalition forces and potential attack strategies to defend their land. The kings may or may not have known about the God of the Israelites, but Jericho's and Ai's destruction were evidence that those desert wanderers were a threat to their land. All of the kings were in, and so were their people. Except for one group.

After hearing about Joshua's victory at Jericho and Ai, the people of Gibeon decided to forgo joining the other kings and try to save themselves. Here's a question: Why did they assume that they needed to save themselves? This is the first clue that there was more than meets the eye with this group. We'll get back to that later.

After hearing about what had happened to the people of Jericho and Ai, the Gibeonites weren't so sure that Joshua would be interested in pardoning them for their association with the conquered peoples. They decided to create a deceptive story, complete with costumes and props.

When a group of ambassadors from different cities in Gibeon arrived with a dubious plan, the Israelites questioned the delegation and warned them that if they lived close by, then a treaty wasn't possible. But the savvy Hivites had come prepared with quite a story. They told Joshua and the other leaders that they had traveled a long way to make a peace treaty with the Israelites. As evidence of their long journey, the men held up cracked wineskins and moldy bread and showed off their tattered clothes. I love how they embellished their story: "This bread was hot from the ovens when we left our homes. But now, as you can see, it is dry and moldy" (Joshua 9:12).

After looking at all the evidence, the Israelites made their decision.

Based on what they saw, the Israelites believed what the travelers had to say. Yet, the Scriptures reveal a critical omission that would cost them dearly later: "The Israelites examined their food, but they did not consult the Lord" (v. 14).

Not only did Joshua and the Israelites neglect to consult God, but they also violated one of God's expressed commands. They sinned by entering into a treaty, which God had specifically prohibited: "But listen carefully to everything I command you today. Then I will go ahead of you and drive out the Amorites, Canaanites, Hittites, Perizzites, Hivites, and Jebusites. Be very careful never to make a treaty with the people who live in the land where you are going. If you do, you will follow their evil ways and be trapped" (Exodus 34:11-12).

Joshua and the leaders entered into a treaty anyway. Then they decided to do a follow-up investigation and discovered that the delegation lived just a few days' journey away. When the Israelites found out about the treaty, they were quite upset, but they didn't kill the Gibeonites. Instead, they put them into service.

Why did the Gibeonites lie? Joshua asked the delegation this very question, and their answer sounds strikingly similar to Rahab's proclamation to the two spies at Jericho: "We...were clearly told that the Lord your God commanded his servant Moses to give you this entire land and to destroy all the people living in it. So we feared greatly for our lives because of you. That is why we have done this" (Joshua 9:24).

Like Rahab, the Gibeonites had heard of God's deeds and they believed in God's power to give the Israelites the land. This is what we call faith. Now, the Gibeonites were deceptive and their lies had severe consequences. But they did believe.

Ultimately, Joshua made a mistake here. He didn't consult God. As a result, the Gibeonites' fear and resulting deception ended up as his ongoing problem.

A Healthy Alternative to Secondhand Worry

Love is sacrificial but not suicidal. You don't need to put your life at risk in order to rescue someone else. How can we prevent ourselves from falling into secondhand worry like Joshua? Since we've already learned the difference between worry and concern, we can carry forward that wisdom to dealing with others who are struggling or in crisis. We want to figure out how to support a friend or loved one in a tough situation. It's good to know when your efforts will truly be helpful versus offering "help" that only creates harm. If you've been caught in secondhand worry, you know what it's like to hemorrhage money or spend sleepless nights because someone in your life didn't manage his or her business. I've said it before and I'll say it again: don't let someone else's worry wear you out!

I want to introduce the "Sort-It-Out" tool. Using the acronym LITE, a few questions and a few suggestions can help you determine how you can show love and concern to others without assuming responsibility for their actions or wearing their worry.

These following questions are a simple rubric, and I've put key words in parentheses in case you want to memorize shortcuts so that you can apply this tool in the future.

1. Am I legally responsible for this person? (*legal status*)

2. Is this person asking for support in an improving situation or rescue from a self-inflicted AND declining situation? (*improving*)

3. Does this person have a track record of asking others for help or of irresponsible decisions? (*track record*)

4. Will my assistance reinforce this person's self-reliance or make this person more dependent in the future? (*enabling*)

If you answered yes to the first question, then you are bound by the legalities of protecting and providing for that individual. However, you can still apply good boundaries or guidelines to help him or her grow in appropriate responsibility.

If you answered no to the first question but your answers to any one of the following questions is unfavorable, then you may be setting yourself up for secondhand worry after you help this individual. It's not my role to advise you *not* to help but to realize that your helping has the potential to hurt both of you. It's hurting the person asking for help because instead of allowing his or her consequences to push that individual toward God, you might be putting yourself in the way. It's hurting you because you're hefting responsibility for someone who doesn't want to be responsible.

I recognize that the answers to the questions might be complex. No doubt there will be emotions involved. That is why prayer is so important. When you pray, God's wisdom can cut through your emotions and deliver clarity. Furthermore, in prayer, God's Holy Spirit may reveal or remind you of something that wasn't obvious during your conversation with that person.

If you determine that it would not be healthy to aid someone, saying no is difficult, but you've got to do it—both for that person's sake and for yours! Here are a few things that you can say instead of yes:

- "I'm so sorry about your situation, but I am unable to help you at this time."
- "That is so difficult! Can I help you put together a plan that you can use to deal with this situation?" (Only if you can plan without taking responsibility, of course!)
- "I know that you can figure this out. Keep me posted on how you are doing."

It feels bad saying no to helping someone, but remember, you aren't saying that the individual isn't worthy of help, only that you aren't getting in the way of God helping him or her.

There are lots of ways to show support without taking responsibility for someone's situation. Following is a list of go behaviors, which express concern, and a list of no-go behaviors, which reinforce worry:

Go Behaviors
- Listening during a phone call
- Providing a meal
- Praying and/or fasting for the person
- Listening without giving advice
- Sending a card
- Saying no to requests for a bailout

No-Go Behaviors
- Staying up all night fretting and/or crying
- Getting angry
- Giving money that you don't have
- Giving money if the person is a poor money manager
- Launching into long lectures

When it comes to our loved ones, it's so hard to distinguish between helping and hurting, but you can do it.

In the meantime, remember this final thought:
You can show love and concern without letting someone else's worry wear you out.

❦ 15 ❦

Does Your Hurry Cause Worry?

Time flies like an arrow. . . . Fruit flies like a banana.

—Anthony G. Oettinger (*Scientific American*, 1966)

*D*id you know that all of the clocks at Grand Central Terminal in New York City are set one minute ahead? Even more surprising is that the clocks are set ahead on purpose. Instead of conductors yelling for tardy would-be passengers to hurry up, they motion for rushing, panicked future passengers to slow down. As a result, the marble-floored Grand Central Station has the fewest passenger slip-and-fall accidents of any other station in the country. As one writer describes it, "Fast clocks make for slower passengers."[1]

Before auto-synced smartphones, all of the manual clocks in my house and car were set five to ten minutes ahead. On purpose! As one who regular rushed for time, I tried to fool myself into thinking that time was passing faster than it was. It never worked. Since I knew that my clocks were ahead, I considered the space between the fake time and real time as an opportunity to fit more stuff into an already jammed schedule. *Quick! I can toss in one more load of laundry, or if I hurry, I can toss dinner in the slow cooker.*

I can't tell you how many times I've yelled, "I'm running out of time!" Lucy Swindoll nails a dead-on description of many years of my life: "For most of us, our greatest fear is running out of time. So we hurry through life trying desperately to get everything done: working overtime, eating fast food in the car, racing down the freeway. In our quest to save time, we're losing something."[2]

As I reflect on my parenting years, I have very few regrets. But the biggest regret of all was too many years without regular family dinners. Our kids have a lot of awards, and I experienced a lot of career success. But our busy schedules cost us the one daily ritual that I can never get back: sharing a nightly together around the table. I can honestly say that I'd give back the books, my sales and other awards, the kids' achievements, and everything else for a few years of simple, regular meals around our dinner table.

Have you ever heard of *hurry sickness?* Professor Richard Jolly, who has studied managers for more than ten years, defines it as the "constant need to do more, faster, even when there's no objective reason to be in a rush."[3]

This is one of those tender areas where God has done major renovation work in my life, including a career change. I was dying mentally, physically, relationally, and spiritually from a horrible case of hurry sickness. Yet, I insisted that I didn't need treatment. My symptoms were constant stress, a relentless schedule, and lots of missed family moments. I often interrupted my husband, children, or coworkers during meetings, needing them to get to the point quickly so I could say what I needed to say and move on to the next thing. I gave up trying to get to meetings and appointments on time. Once my first meeting ran long, I felt like I could never catch up. It never occurred to me to stand up and say, "I'm so sorry; I need to be on schedule for my next appointment."

Hurry sickness cost me dearly at home. As much as I loved to make dinner for my family, one season of hurry sickness sabotaged my desire and energy to make dinner. I just stopped cooking, which I loved and my family valued. This self-inflicted disease cost me moments with my kids. I couldn't stop and just *be* with them because there was always something else that I elected to do. Hurry sickness was a mental illness that made it easy for me to lie to myself about just how sick I was. *Just one more thing, Barb. If you do this one more thing, you'll be ahead.* So, I'd stay up late writing, planning, or responding to emails.

I've been in recovery for the past few years, but I'm under no delusion that I'm cured. It took years for me to learn that the more to-do's, appointments, or reminders I wrote down, the less time I would have to get everything done.

Is your rushing driven by worry, or is your worry driven by rushing? I feel like both are true in my life. How often do you worry that you'll run out of time before getting everything done in your life? Here are some of the time-pressured worries that we might battle:

We worry that we won't have the money in time.
We worry that he or she won't stay in the relationship long enough.
We worry that the medicine or treatment won't work in time.
We worry that we're not spending enough time with our kids.

Ever since the beginning of the world, we've worried about the limits of time. In God's economy, time is a tool, not a limit. As she dialogues about the 25,550-day bucket of time that the average human gets to live, Ann Voskamp poses the one question that governs

> Is your rushing driven by worry, or is your worry driven by rushing? I feel like both are true in my life.

every day of our lives: "How will you use your time?"[4] Ann says, "It's God hands that control the universe. The hands of the clock are bound by the decisions of our hands. And He has made our hands free to be His."[5]

Since God exists outside of time, He never worries about it like we do. One scriptural author writes about how God holds and controls time for His purposes: "He has made everything beautiful in its time. He has also set eternity in the human heart; yet no one can fathom what God has done from beginning to end" (Ecclesiastes 3:11). Even though we feel pressured by our circumstances or the people around us who seem to be getting ahead, another Scripture author reminds us to surrender our timeline to God's timing. "Be still in the presence of the Lord, and wait patiently for him to act. Don't worry about evil people who prosper or fret about their wicked schemes" (Psalm 37:7).

What's your hurry worry today? The roots for my friend Lauren's began in high school.

> My stomach would be tied up in knots all day long and I'd think, *I have to get this done.* What was I in a hurry over? I don't know. Until recently, I worried my whole life, and that caused me to live in a hurry. Since we moved recently, God has been dealing with me. Hurry is not wholeness. That's not how God designed me to live. I'm working on being wise about what God has called me to do and not do. It's been an important place of growing in faith and trust.[6]

Now when Lauren feels that her gut is getting tied up, that's a signal for her to step back and look at her schedule to remove some obligations from her plate.

God gives us enough time for the things He's called us to do. The problem is that we don't *feel* like we have enough time. How do we back ourselves out of rushing and running all the time in order to stick with the tasks that God has given us?

God Never Hurries

Let's go back to the battlefield as Joshua runs into a *not-enough-time* problem and God shows up with a *time-is-not-an-issue* answer.

In Joshua 10, the Israelites are chasing after the five Amorite kings and soldiers who've attacked the city of Gibeon. The kings were afraid that the alliance between Gibeon and the Israelites could be problematic for their cities because Gibeon had a lot of resources, including skilled warriors.

Under siege, Gibeon sent messengers to Joshua, pleading for help. Before the Israelites took their first step toward coming to Gibeon's aid, God gave Joshua a promise of victory over the Amorite kings: "Do not be afraid of them, for I have given you victory over them. Not a single one of them will be able to stand up to you" (v. 8).

Joshua and the Israelites marched all night long toward Gibeon. Not only did the Israelites catch the Amorites in the early morning hours by surprise, but God provided supernatural aid by raining down hailstones to pummel the Amorite soldiers. In fact, hailstones kill more enemy soldiers than the Israelites did with their swords.

As the battle continued, Joshua and his fighting men chased their enemies over the hills, valleys, and roadways. As God had promised, the Israelites trounced the enemy soldiers, yet Joshua sensed that they would not finish the job before dark, when fighting would end for the night. It would be bad to accidentally stab one of his own soldiers because he couldn't see in the darkness. With that in mind, Joshua uttered one of the boldest prayers ever recorded in history. In front of the entire army, Joshua prayed, "Let the sun stand still over Gibeon and the moon over the valley of Aijalon" (v. 12).

Of all of the things that he could pray for, why did Joshua ask God to make the sun stand still? It's here that we learn a lot about Joshua as a leader. We also learn three important life lessons that we can use in our own lives:

153

1. You need to stay and fight until the battle is over or God calls you away from it.
2. When you're on mission for God, He's waiting for you to ask for the impossible.
3. God never runs out of time to do the impossible.

First, notice how Joshua didn't pray for God to finish the battle for him or to drop the enemy soldiers dead in their tracks. As a warrior on mission, Joshua was willing to fight until the battle was over.

I don't want to run away from the fights in my life. I want to fight in faith and claim God's victory over the circumstances that cause me to worry or battle the imaginations that try to influence my peace of mind.

Does Joshua's prayer inspire you to pray your own "sun stand still" prayer? In his book *Sun Stand Still*, Steven Furtick describes Joshua's kind of faith as audacious, which is bold or daring.[7] Then he challenges us with a question: "Does the brand of faith you live by produce the kinds of results in your life that you read about in the biblical stories of men and women of faith?"[8]

Have you ever prayed a prayer as bold as Joshua did on that day? He asked God to do the impossible, and God did it—except, of course, that the task *wasn't* impossible for God. As Jesus would tell us, "Humanly speaking, it is impossible. But with God everything is possible" (Matthew 19:26).

What has God called you to do that's impossible on your own?

Have you ever witnessed what happens when you pray and God begins to change the heart of someone far from Him into an on-fire believer? A transformed human life is just as powerful as the sun standing still for a day.

Sister, God is still answering "sun stand still" prayers! The question that you must ask is, Am I willing to pray one?

Take a moment and speak your "sun stand still" prayer to God about something in your life that seems so impossible, yet you know with God it is possible.

How easy or difficult was that prayer for you? It's far easier for us to imagine the worst of the worst of our worries than to dream of God's ability to do the impossible. I love Priscilla Shirer's word on this: "If you really believe what God has said about His unlimited ability, then guess what? You may have prayed your last, undersized prayer for the rest of your life, both for yourself and others."[9]

My "sun stand still" prayer was: *God, I feel You calling me away from my current job and lifestyle into a different place. But You know that there's no way that I can do this on my own. If it's gonna get done, You're going to have to do it.*

Praying those types of prayers is tough! That bold prayer reveals our rawest desires. Furthermore, as soon as our hearts open to pray with such boldness, worry tries to invade that soft, vulnerable space to make us doubt God's ability or desire to answer. Yet we pray in faith anyway, because God will answer.

How did God answer Joshua's prayer? "So the sun stood still and the moon stayed in place until the nation of Israel had defeated its enemies. The sun stayed in the middle of the sky, and it did not set as on a normal day. There has never been a day like this one before or since, when the Lord answered such a prayer. Surely the Lord fought for Israel that day" (Joshua 10:13-14).

The long day account is one of those most debated stories in the Bible. Historians and scientists contest this story, and skeptics use this account as one of their main arguments for why the Bible can't be true. Faith doesn't require us to throw out our brains, but we should also remember that if God is capable of anything, then making the sun stand still for a day isn't going to tax His capacity. Still there are a few possibilities that could explain how the sun could have stood still:

Possibility #1: The earth actually stopped rotating. Natural laws would have been thrown into chaos, but God would have managed any fallout from such a disruption.

Possibility #2: God employed a miracle of refraction. The earth continued to rotate, but God created a mirage so that it appeared that the sun was still out.

Possibility #3: The earth slowed but didn't stop. God slowed the earth's rotation to a speed that would last an additional day.[10]

These are just a few possibilities, but I encourage you to check out the research for yourself. God's not afraid of your skepticism or your questions. We're supposed to study for ourselves and ask God to help us find the answers.

For all of the debate about the long day account, what is the biggest takeaway for you and me? There will always be enough time for what God has called us to do.

How to Halt Your Hurry

A few years ago, I read a quotation that sent a shockwave through my life. In his book *Soulkeeping*, John Ortberg had a series of conversations with philosopher Dallas Willard. After moving to Chicago and beginning a challenging new assignment, Ortberg called Willard to ask about how to stay healthy spiritually. It was during that conversation that Willard uttered a sentence that God would use to radically change my life: "You must ruthlessly eliminate hurry from your life."[11]

Now, that sentence may not mean much to you, but it was a bullet that found its mark in the heart of the biggest challenge of my life. I lost track of what *God was calling me to do* because I was always thinking about *what I thought I had to do*. God used those words to finally pivot me toward a new, slower speed of life.

I don't know what your hurry is about, but I've been around a lot of hurriers and seen some similar grouped characteristics. Some people hurry because they think everyone needs them and there's not enough of them to go around. Others hurry because they're frustrated perfectionists who can't finish tasks. Some high-capacity hurriers can do a lot, but neglect to prioritize, so they're always at Mach 5, with their hair on fire. I don't know if any of those categories resonates with you, but at different phases of my life, I fell into all of those categories and sometimes, I fell into two categories at once.

How did I stop the insanity? First, let me say that I'm still recovering, and it will likely always be that way. I know me, and I like shiny objects that promise the sparkle of amazing, exciting, and challenging. Yet, there has been one very helpful and simple tool that I've used to practically slow down my hurry while I grappled with the bigger spiritual issues behind the "why" of my hurry.

My practical tip is to make sure that there is at least an hour in between appointments or obligations on my calendar. Why an hour? That leaves time for the previous meeting to run ten minutes over without making me late for the next one. It leaves time for me to drive at a regular speed across town instead of screaming at stoplights.

Once I began scheduling with a one-hour buffer, I also began limiting the number of appointments, errands, or phone calls I scheduled each day. For a woman whose philosophy used to be "I'll fit it in," this was a radical new way of living with a margin that felt like a thrill one moment and cheating the next.

My journey to remain in recovery from hurry follows along the framework of these four words:

- *Conviction.* What is my role at home and work in this season of my life?
- *Clarity.* What are the things that only I can do at home or in my job?
- *Creativity.* What are the unique gifts and talents that I want or need to use in this season of life?
- *Connection.* Which relationships is God calling me to prioritize?

Answering these questions allows me to look at my daily schedule and identify time stealers.

There are lots of great books and wonderful Bible studies out there on the topics of being overwhelmed, slowing down, finding simplicity, and rest. So, if this topic rings your bell, make sure to follow through on finding a study and really immersing yourself in God's Word on that topic.

Here's how we'll wrap this up:
A hurry-free life goes a long way toward a worry-free life.

16

How to Slay All Day

> We have to fight them daily, like fleas, those many small worries
> about the morrow, for they sap our energies.
>
> —Etty Hillesum

O n one flight home, I tapped my foot at my gate while watching my cell phone battery level drop lower and lower. I needed my phone to stay alive because I needed to show the gate staff my mobile boarding pass to board the plane and fly home. It was my own fault that my phone battery was at 1 percent because I forgot to plug it in the night before. In fact, I often forget to plug in my phone at night. There are many reasons why I forget, and none of them matter when I'm standing in a line, hoping my phone charge lasts long enough for me to show my boarding pass and get on my plane.

Whenever I have one of those my-phone's-gonna-die moments, I'm reminded that if I'm not careful with how I use my personal energy battery, I may feel like I'm gonna die too.

Our daily energy is the capacity to get things done.[1] As a visual, our energy for life looks our cell phone batteries. You know that your phone battery drains faster or slower based on how much or how little you use your phone. The more we use our phones, the faster the batteries decline. The more open apps on our phones, the faster our batteries die.

Did you know that you can see what's draining your battery each day on your phone? I go to my phone's settings and get to see which apps drain my battery, as well as how much time I use my phone each day. I've started paying attention to the dozen apps that only use 1 percent but are draining my phone's energy in the background. (While I was typing this, I picked up my phone and closed nineteen screens in the background.)

The background issues in our lives can drain our energy without us realizing it. Can you think of some of the background issues of your life that might be draining your daily energy? Here's a list of energy drainers:

- unhealed hurts from your past or present
- active relational conflict
- unmanaged mental, emotional, or physical pain
- grief
- unresolved spiritual questions or conflict with God
- addiction

For example, you could begin the day feeling great. Then your mom calls and her conversation brings up your parents' divorce when you were a kid. Now you remember the pain of watching your dad pack up and storm out and all of the back-and-forth between houses. Even though the divorce happened years before, the emotions of that painful time wash fresh over you again. Before talking to your mom, you might have been planning to run errands or paint your living room. Now you're tired and want to take a nap.

Those battery-draining background issues stay open and keep draining your energy until you deal with them.

Battery drains can also happen with good things! If you've moved, had a baby, gotten a promotion, launched a business, or built a home, you know that those life events can wear you down. My daily work in ministry gives me the opportunity to travel, write, and speak. I love it! But I've learned to be aware of my personal battery each day. I used to drain my personal batteries all the time, but now I'm learning how to keep myself from becoming completely drained.

Do you want to stay recharged when it comes to fighting your worry battle each day? I'm pretty sure that your answer is yes, but I know that some of you are worried that you're going to fall back into old patterns of behavior. So, I'm excited about tackling the tough challenge that Christians run into when it comes to developing a long-term, winning strategy to fight not only a worry battle, but any other life challenge that tries to rob us of God's victory in every area of our life.

Killing the Kings of Worry

When Joshua prayed his "sun stand still" prayer (Joshua 10), God kept the sun in place for an entire day so Israel's soldiers could fight until the enemy soldiers were all defeated. Can you imagine fighting for a twenty-four-hour period? Put yourself in the position of one of those soldiers. It's tiring enough doing a thirty-minute workout! Imagine the physical exertion of chasing, swinging swords, and wrestling as being equivalent to running almost six 26.2-mile marathons in one day. It wasn't as if the soldiers on either side could clock out for a coffee break, eat lunch, or use the bathroom.

What did it take for those men to fight all day? Training. They didn't have horses or chariots but rather their swords, their smarts, and their commitment to fight. They knew that God would give them victory over their enemies, but those men still stayed out on the battlefield for as long as it took to win.

While the Israelites fought, Joshua received word that the five enemy kings were hiding in a cave. Rather than move his troops away from their current battle, Joshua kept his troops on task, but instructed some soldiers to put a large stone in front of the cave to trap the kings.

After the battle was over, Joshua commanded his leaders to bring the kings out of the cave. I don't know how long the kings were trapped in the cave, but they would not have been excited about seeing that stone removed.

What happened next is a unique object lesson that Joshua offered to his soldiers. Remember, these men had battled for an entire day. No doubt they were tired, perhaps even a little "hangry" over a few missed meals. But Joshua gave them an opportunity of a lifetime. The men would never forget what happened next.

Joshua commanded his soldiers to put their feet on the necks of the once-powerful kings. Imagine how it might have felt for a lowly army private to put his boot on the neck of the president of one of our country's enemies. The kings' necks were vulnerable to getting crushed or even snapped every time an Israelite soldier raised his foot.

Think about the mixture of awe and excitement those soldiers must have felt. The defeated kings were not only humiliated by their capture and terror over their likely deaths, but I'm pretty sure they smelled a lot of stinky Israelite soldier feet.

Next, Joshua added an exclamation point on that powerful moment by addressing his men with the very words that God had spoken to him many times before: "Don't be afraid or terrified. Be brave and strong, because this is how the Lord will deal with all the enemies you fight" (Joshua 10:25 CEB). I can see Joshua speaking these words with as much conviction as anything that he's ever said to his troops, and in that moment, Joshua cast a prophetic vision for his men that stretched far beyond their present and into their future.

We've used a lot of different visual imagery to describe worry, but this one is compelling because we all have powerful worries that, like the enemy kings, fuel the other struggles and worries we have in life. Those giant worries are often attached to the background issues that drain us each day.

God calls us to trust Him during the hard fight to deal with or find healing from those background issues in our lives. It's hard work letting go of stinky baggage or learning to forgive. Yet, when we stay in the fight and God brings us through, He invites us put our feet across the neck of what previously tried to hold us captive or kill us. If you look at 2 Samuel 22:40, Psalm 18:39, and Psalm 110:1, we're told that God will subdue our enemies under our feet.

Take a moment and think about what it could mean for your life to no longer experience the hardship or heartache associated with baggage. Not only will you snap the neck of its power over you, but you will cut off its ability to generate worry in your life, too.

Cue a Lasting Victory

Having the energy to slay worry doesn't happen naturally. Sometimes, we don't feel like fighting, but we've got to create a habit to overcome how we feel in the moment.

Some individuals hate routine and habits, while others cheer for them. For most of us, worry became a habit at some point in our lives. As we learn life lessons and tools, we're in the process of doing something different, but we've got to put two helpful features in place so that our new warrior ways can become habits.

In his best-selling book, *The Power of Habit*, author Charles Duhigg talks about how we focus on the behavior that we want to change, but the success of that behavior change depends on the cue and reward associated with the change. A cue is a trigger that prompts the desired behavior. A reward reinforces the good feelings associated with the behavior. Cues and rewards are essential in helping you keep a lock on fighting your long-term worry battle. They help you establish the routines that will support your fighting-in-faith training as well as position you for God's victory.

At the time of this writing, my daughter Abbie is on a one-hundred-plus-day Snapchat streak with my niece Kayla. Each morning both girls send each other a Snapchat. Both are still in bed and barely awake when they snap, but they do it any way. What are they snapping and sending? "Sometimes, I send a picture of the wall," Abbie replied.

I asked why the girls were so intent upon their daily snaps. She shrugged and replied that they had an even longer daily streak the year before. Now they wanted to see if they could beat it. While those two beautiful girls think they're just sending daily snaps, they demonstrate the power of cues and rewards.

In this example, what was their cue or trigger to start the behavior? Simply waking up. What's their behavior? They exchange snaps. What's their reward? Just the feeling of accomplishment for continuing their streak one more day.

Have you identified the rewards of winning your worry battle in a narrow sense or the more important and greater purpose of following God? Too many Christians think about their "Christian duty," but that phrase doesn't inspire us to joy or fulfillment, only to a sense of obligation, like going to the dentist twice a year. We don't get excited about obligation.

Romans 12:2 paints a more satisfying picture for us: "Don't copy the behavior and customs of this world, but let God transform you into a new person by changing the way you think. Then you will learn to know God's will for you, which is good and pleasing and perfect." God wants to literally make us new by removing old ways of thinking and replacing them with His ways, but do we get excited about that?

Probably not as much as we should. Notice the words associated with allowing God's way of life to flow through you: *good, pleasing,* and *perfect.* Doesn't this sound like the kind of life that you want to live? It does to me!

As a longtime church staffer in spiritual development ministry, I developed all kinds of spiritual growth resources. For over ten years, I led a team that created a weekly five-day Bible study for our church. However, the tension was finding the secret sauce to get people to actually do the five-day study each week.

First, we tackled creating a cue. We delivered the Bible study via email each day. When people saw their email, it prompted them to open and engage with the study. Email delivery was a good cue, but the reward was a little harder to figure out.

Throughout the years that I led the team, a man named Jack would find me a few times a year and show me his binder filled with the weekly Bible studies. When his binder filled up, he'd take them out and start collecting them again. Jack had Bible studies dating back more than ten years. It was impressive! For Jack, his reward was looking at the Bible studies and experiencing the sense of accomplishment in completing them each week.

Jack's accomplishment went deeper than just completing a weekly Bible study. He'll tell you all about how much God has changed his heart and life because he had a weekly study habit.

Cues and rewards aren't about helping you accomplish a behavior for the behavior's sake. They are to motivate and inspire you beyond the behavior you seek. If you lose twenty-five pounds, you're going to be excited about the number on the scale, but you're going to be more excited about your increased health, better-fitting clothes, and sense of accomplishment. It isn't just about losing weight.

Why do you need cues and rewards for your worry battle? Again, you've got a list of tools that you can use whenever a few eight-legged worries crawl your way, but what will trigger you to pull out one of those tools? Have you experienced a reward that makes you want to pull out a tool that you've learned?

Whether we admit it or not, worry rewards us. It gives us the feeling that we're doing something about our problem, even though we're not. How do we distinguish between the short-term reward that worry offers and the true and lasting reward of fighting in faith?

The two greatest rewards that have come from my worry battle are serenity and self-control. I can trace my behaviors toward putting me in position for God to give me peace, courage, and strength. Every day, I experience the joy of a calm heart, mind, and soul, even as uncertainty swirls around my life. Likewise, I feel such a sense of accomplishment when I am able to hold my tongue from saying unkind words and manage my impulses when it comes emotional eating.

Those rewards are the fruit of victory. When I fight in faith, those rewards are part of the personalized and realized victory that God has given to me. They, like the crowns we'll receive in heaven one day, aren't for me to claim as my own, but to point to as evidence of God's power and presence in my life.

My strategy to stay recharged emotionally, physically, and spiritually was inspired by Mark 12:30: "You must love the Lord your God with all your heart, all your soul, all your mind, and all your strength." Since God is the source of love and all that is in life, I figured that I want to align myself with Him as much as possible. So, here's why my morning routine looks like in this season of my life. It might be different in another season, but this has been in place the past couple of years.

Please know that this is my routine, but God wants you to seek Him to figure out what He's called you to do. I just want to give you a helpful example:

Cue: Trigger for Behavior	Behavior/Habit	Reward: Reinforces Behavior
FitBit 6 a.m. alarm (Get up by 6:20 a.m.)	Workout	Feeling of accomplishment and management of back issue
Workout finished	Walk dog	Enjoy fresh air and walking Clears head Personal growth from listening to podcasts
Finish walking dog	Make breakfast	Taking care of family feels good.
Quiet house	Bible Study/prayer	Love holding my cup of hot chai tea

You'll see that some of the cues and rewards are connected to one another. Let me just say that these are the cues and rewards that work for me. Also, perfect execution isn't the goal. Sometimes I work out for forty-five minutes, and other times I barely survive twenty. If I'm running behind, the dog might only get a five-minute walk instead of thirty minutes. Breakfast could be cereal and a "Let's go!" There are times when I'm antsy during my Bible study and prayer and have to come back to them later. At the end of every routine, I enjoy a cup of hot chai tea with my Bible study and prayer. In fact, it's the sweet taste and sensory enjoyment of the tea that best motivates me each morning, because I don't like to get out of bed.

Now it's your turn. Work through the following framework to think about the cues, behaviors/habits, and rewards that you need for your worry battle to stay effective. There's an example in for you:

Cue: Trigger for Behavior	Behavior/Habit	Reward: Reinforces Behavior
Brush teeth	Read five Scripture promises written on note card in bathroom	Feeling of accomplishment and spiritual strength

I want you to be equipped to fight in faith every day for the rest of your life. God wants to give you victory, but you don't want failed good intentions to get in the way of receiving it.

Here's a cautionary word from James 1:22-23: "But be sure you live out the message and do not merely listen to it and so deceive yourselves. For if someone merely listens to the message and does not live it out, he is like someone who gazes at his own face in a mirror. For he gazes at himself and then goes out and immediately forgets what sort of person he was" (NET).

We cannot live out the message of the Scriptures unless we adopt and absorb it into our lives. Don't put your faith in good intentions. Stop saying that you'll try to read your Bible more or pray more. You can do better than that, and best of all, God can help you do better than that!

Here's a final thought:
We learn to slay when we train each day.

∾ 17 ∾

Secret Weapon

"Blessed are those who hunger and thirst for righteousness, for they shall be satisfied."

—Matthew 5:6 ESV

What do you do if you've got hard-core worry that won't budge? The kind of worry that's stuck to you like Gorilla Glue and no matter how much you've read your Bible or prayed, that automatic worry won't budge? Perhaps you can relate to this story:

> I think that this is something I have yet to be able to "solve" or figure out how to deal with it. Lately my worry has been more out of control than ever. It isn't going away, but I still get up with a smile every morning, pray, follow my daily routine and remember that life will always give you worry, even of it is just about the slight pain from the paper cut in your finger to a car or house that need unaffordable repairs. Trying not to let my emotions and brain and thoughts take over my existence.

Can you relate to this person? It feels like a double whammy to both be a Christian *and* feel like a failure because you can't stop worry.

If I could describe how I felt during my toughest worry years, I'd describe myself as a "holy hot mess." I'd be praying one minute and panicking the next. That constant yo-yo made me feel like a crazy person. This is a hard kind of hot mess to be because I constantly lived in guilt because I just wasn't shaking this worry problem. In a previous chapter, I mentioned that I'm also a control freak worrier, which at least partially explains my habits and behaviors. But I needed to figure out what was going on deep inside of me.

There were some places of worry in my mind that I could describe as being like a deep dental plaque that just wouldn't budge. While it's good to brush our teeth every day, sometimes the most stubborn plaque remains. Periodically, we need to go to the dentist's office because a dentist has tools that we don't have access to in order to remove the damaging dental plaque that our toothbrushes can't.

For me, every visit to the dentist starts off great until the hygienist picks up the dental pick. At that point, I stop smiling and preemptively grip the chair's armrests. Nothing has touched my mouth yet and I'm already anticipating the pain of what is to come. As the sharp-tipped hook of the tool moves toward my mouth, I fight the urge to jump out of the chair and run away. I hate the sound and feeling of those short scrapes raking against my teeth. Still, I also know that the hygienist's expert hand will guide that tool into the deep crevices and clean out the microparticles that can destroy not only tissue and enamel but also my overall health.

Do you want to learn about a "secret weapon" that God will use like a dental hook to scrape out the stubborn, insidious, we-ain't-coming-out worry in your life? At first you won't be able to see what God is doing. However, this weapon is a game changer with the power to radically shift the trajectory of your worry problem from struggle to success.

So, what is this secret weapon that can radically change your worry battle? In a word, *fasting*, that is, to "abstain from all or some kinds of food or drink, especially as a religious observance."[1]

How do you feel or think about fasting? Which answer best matches you:

1. I don't know much about it.
2. I'm intimidated/uncomfortable just thinking about it.
3. I've tried fasting, and it was not a good experience.
4. I've fasted in the past, but it's been a while.
5. I engage in periodic or regular fasting.

Personally, I hated this tool for many years of my life because I just didn't want to do it. Like going to the dentist, I didn't want to deal with any discomfort. However, in my effort to avoid discomfort, I didn't allow God access to the deepest, darkest places of steadfast worry in my life.

I felt good about avoiding fasting until I'd answered the questions that kept me from fasting. *What's so spiritual about skipping a meal? What if I can't do it? Will God be mad at me if I start a fast and can't finish it?*

Yet, God's kindness gently led me toward where I didn't want to go. First, God placed my friend Lauri in my life many years ago to cast a vision for regular weekly fasting. She fasted every Wednesday. Lauri never boasted of her fasting, but spoke of it as an opportunity for focused prayer. Over the years, I tried fasting periodically until a season of my life when my worry skyrocketed into the stratosphere. That new worry battle was either going to destroy me or create an opportunity for a new perspective on discipleship where I allowed God to reshape and remold me in a radical new way.

I share my story with you because you might be struggling with the idea of fasting. It's okay if you feel intimidated at the thought of skipping a meal. It's even okay if you're saying, "No way" to abstaining from food the entire day. Trust me; I've been there. Fasting is not just for people who seem to be "super-Christians"; rather, it is a secret weapon that amplifies our connection to God in new and powerful ways.

God wants what's best for you, even if you aren't ready for it yet. Romans 2:4 tells us that it's God's kindness that leads us to repentance. Instead of beating yourself up for not wanting to fast or not following through when you do, remember that God cares about helping you feel closer to Him, not getting you to follow a bunch of rules.

The Greek word for "repentance" is *metanoia,* which means "a change of mind."[2] Just as God lovingly and gently reshaped my heart on the topic of fasting, He will do the same for you, but only if you want Him to.

Fasting can be intimidating, but we're going to see how fasting can strip away all of our human facades. When we fast, it provides an opportunity for God to get to the core of what chases us, tempts us, or keeps us from experiencing victory in our lives.

A Hungry Day in the Desert

Comfort food used to be a staple in my life. Whenever I felt stressed or worried, I could always count on creamy dips, homemade brownies, or barbecue potato chips to help me feel better. Those comfort foods worked, but only for a little while. Unfortunately, the consequences of my comfort food stuck with me for much longer.

Jesus also faced a situation when Satan wanted Him to depend on food instead of God for survival.

In Matthew 4, Jesus had begun His ministry in a small town near a desert that stretched for dozens of miles from the Jordan Valley west toward Jerusalem. His ministry was launched right after His baptism, which was a mountaintop experience that would have been a highlight of His human life experience. Then, in the first verse of chapter 4, we read that God's Spirit took Jesus to the desert to be tempted by the devil.

Think about what it must have been like for Jesus in the desert. There he was fully exposed to harsh desert weather conditions with no protection from wild animals. And there were no friends to call and no soft place to lay His head.

In addition to facing the desert backdrop, Jesus also fasted for forty days and forty nights. Can you imagine going all that time without food? In the early days when I tried to fast, it only took about three or four hours before I felt like I might fall out onto the floor and die. In this case, Jesus fasted for more than a month. If we calculate based on our Western diet, Jesus fasted from 120 meals. And we think we'll die after skipping just one meal.

Then, after all of that time without food, the devil shows up. Note to self: Satan will always show up whenever you're on the battlefield. He knows that God will give you the victory. Satan is there to discourage you so that you'll give up before you receive it.

Why did God's Spirit lead Jesus into the wilderness to be tempted? It seems harsh that God would send Jesus into sensual depravation and spiritual temptation. But God did this so that we could see how the power of God living within us can help us overcome our human desires that can get out of control. We get to see how Jesus's dependence on God empowered him not only to face tremendous human physical and emotional stress but also to withstand a severe test of His spiritual fortitude.[3]

If your worry is stuck on out-of-control or you're worried that you might fall back into worry after experiencing some victory, then you might draw encouragement from what Jesus experienced, both the struggle against his hunger as well as His ability to withstand temptation.

They say that the way to a man's heart is through his stomach. Thankfully, Jesus proves that this isn't always the case. When the devil showed up to tempt Jesus, he appealed to Jesus's hunger: "If you are the Son of God, tell these stones to become loaves of bread" (Matthew 4:3).

When I read this verse, it's not hard for me to imagine Satan holding a platter of fresh, hot bread with rich, melted butter slowly rolling down the sides. I can almost smell the yeasty aroma wafting through the air and floating under Jesus's nose. Did Satan hope that Jesus would rationalize a reason to convert the stones on the ground into a hot, filling meal that could satisfy His hunger but scald His soul?

As a woman who has dealt with emotional eating as a way to cope with stress and worry, I find that Jesus's response in verse 4 ministers to my soul. For many years, snacks smoothed over my worries and struggles. But here's what Jesus said: "People do not live by bread alone, but by every word that comes from the mouth of God."

Jesus's response was actually quoted from an address that Moses gave in Deuteronomy 8. At the time, the Israelites were hungry and begging God for food. So, God provided manna to satisfy their physical hunger and teach them dependence upon Him. While our Israelite sister was in the wilderness, she had to look to the heavens each day for the food that kept her and her family alive.

Jesus's response to Satan reveals an essential need in my life. I can't deal with my worry until I learn how to depend on God. It wasn't until I fasted that I realized how often I sought comfort and security in other places instead of in God. When I fast from food or social media, I sense their absence from my life in powerful ways. I realize how often my mind is occupied with what I'm eating, planning to eat, or just finished eating, and I get a sobering reality check regarding just how often I blindly grab my phone and access one of my social media accounts.

For some context, fasting isn't a contemporary problem. In fact, on March 30, 1863, President Abraham Lincoln proclaimed that April 30 would be a National Fast Day. At the time, America was not yet highly developed but was instead deeply divided over the Civil War. At a time of great uncertainty and difficulty, Lincoln wrote:

> We have been the recipients of the choicest bounties of Heaven. We have been preserved, these many years, in peace and prosperity. We have grown in numbers, wealth and power, as no other nation has ever grown. But we have forgotten God. We have forgotten the gracious hand which preserved us in peace, and multiplied and enriched and strengthened us; and we have vainly imagined, in the deceitfulness of our hearts, that all these blessings were produced by some superior wisdom and virtue of our own. Intoxicated with unbroken success, we have become too self-sufficient to feel the necessity of redeeming and preserving grace, too proud to pray to the God that made us![4]

It's been more than 150 years since those words were authored, and yet, they could have been written for our country or maybe even for our individual lives today.

Think about how much focus you direct toward food, whether you are a clean eater, a cookie eater, or a calorie counter. What about all of the time we lose while surfing social media? When we voluntarily abstain from those in our lives, it doesn't take long for us to become uncomfortable with their absence as well as unsettled over the fact that we are so uncomfortable without them. Richard Foster sums it up so well: "More than any other discipline, fasting reveals what controls us."[5]

Jesus's example of fasting isn't just something that we can read and admire; it points to the pattern of fasting that should be a part of every believer's life. In Matthew 6:16, Jesus began His teaching on fasting with the phrase, "When you fast…" To be clear, fasting isn't just a Christian thing; religions throughout time have used fasting for spiritual purposes.[6]

Sometimes people get confused about whether or not Christians should fast. Jesus's teaching on fasting emphasizes what not to do while fasting, but it doesn't discourage fasting itself. Here's what Jesus says about fasting:

> And when you fast, don't make it obvious, as the hypocrites do, for they try to look miserable and disheveled so people will admire them for their fasting. I tell you the truth, that is the only reward they will ever get. But when you fast, comb your hair and wash your face. Then no one will notice that you are fasting, except your Father, who knows what you do in private. And your Father, who sees everything, will reward you. (Matthew 6:16-18)

Pharisees in Jesus's time used fasting as a public way to draw attention. They wanted people to see them wasting away as a symbol that they were uber-spiritual. That type of fasting doesn't honor God. Neither does fasting with the attitude that if you're going to give up meals, then God will give you what you want.

As much as Jesus tells us what not to do, He also directs us toward the posture that positions us for our maximum spiritual blessing.

Using Fasting as a Secret Weapon

First, let me say that there is nothing sinful about food.

Also, fasting doesn't make you spiritually superior to anyone else.

Another thing: fasting without prayer is just going hungry.

Finally, fasting doesn't garner God's favor for what you want. It's a spiritual discipline where you allow God to get at the deep-down, stuck-on worry in your life and start to dig it out.

As difficult as it is for me to submit to a weekly fast, this discipline has helped me to, as Spartan CEO Joe DeCena calls it, "train for adversity." I was speaking at an event where DeCena told us how every morning he does three hundred burpees (a squat with a kick back to a plank and back up again) and takes a cold shower. Why does he do this? He says that beginning each morning with two difficult physical tasks increases his threshold for difficulty. He finds that the more he trains for adversity, the less the small stuff bothers him.

When I heard him explain "training for adversity,"[7] that's when I realized how God used the discipline of fasting in my life. Whenever I've chosen to deny myself something that I often use to indulge my selfish desires and combine that with increase focused on God, I've had greater success in controlling my words and fighting selfish impulses.

My weekly fast begins on Tuesday after dinner and ends with breakfast on Thursday. I refrain from solid foods and I drink water, tea, juice, broth, or coffee. Generally, I arrange my schedule around my fast so that I don't bring public attention to it. This means that I try to avoid scheduling lunch or dinner meetings on Wednesdays. However, I'm not rigid about my weekly fast. There are rare occasions when a priority pops up that will prompt me to fast another day of the week.

On my weekly fast day, I begin with expressing my desire to allow God to use the day to speak specifically to my heart and mind, as well reveal what I need to repent or confess.

Practically speaking, I get up and dressed like any other day, but I modify my workout since I won't be consuming replacement calories afterward.

I still make meals for my family, even cooking bacon (which I love!). My work doesn't change much on fast day. I devote myself to a full day of work, whether writing, prepping for a speaking engagement, or meeting with coaching clients. No one knows what I'm doing but God. However, I know that what God is doing in me is transforming my heart, mind, and soul at the deepest levels.

Hunger sharpens my senses, and as Richard Foster says, fasting surfaces the hidden, ugly parts of my heart and sends me clambering toward God for sustaining grace. I learn how to lean into God while not bowing to my physical hunger. I also wait for God to nourish the places of my spiritual poverty.

Prayer is essential to my fasting experience. I know that it takes ten to fifteen minutes for me to eat each meal, so I aim to spend that extra time in prayer on my fast day. Some of you can pray for thirty minutes at a clip, but prayer is a discipline that takes a lot of work for me. However, on my fast day, it's an intentional day of discipline when I interrupt my natural go-go-go tendencies to just be-be-be before God in prayer.

Over the past few years, I've seen how God has used fasting in my life to break down my hard-to-manage control issues, as well as teach me dependence upon Him. Since my fast day has an emphasis on prayer, one of the greatest blessings is greater access to my fighting friends, peace, courage, and strength, as well as more self-discipline and patience.

Using the Secret Weapon Well

Even as I've been fasting regularly for several years now, I still have to remain focused on God in order to make it through the day. While I still fight off food desires and a little crankiness, what I've seen is how God has used this secret weapon to give me some incredible victories over worry. Here are some suggestions to help you as you consider fasting:

1. Identify why you need to fast.

Campus Crusade founder Bill Bright wrote a classic guide to fasting.[8] In it he points to a variety of reasons for engaging in a biblical fast, such as the need for spiritual renewal, for guidance, for healing, for resolution of a problem, or for additional grace to handle a tough situation.

Are any of these needs active in your life right now? If you're looking to use fasting as a secret weapon against an aversion to fasting, then that would certainly fall under the need for spiritual renewal or for resolution of a problem.

2. Determine the type of fast.

Pray and ask God what type of fast you should do. While God may not speak audibly to you, perhaps you might sense a leading from God about whether you should fast from food (whether all solid food or certain types of food), devices, or any other compulsion that occupies your thoughts.

3. Determine the length of your fast.

Once you figure out what you are fasting from, then determine how long you should fast. Again, pray and ask God to give you insight. In his fasting guide, Bright covers all types of fasts, from digital fasts to forty-day, water-only fasts. The ultimate decision should come from a conviction born in prayer. If prayer doesn't provide clarity, talk with a trusted Christian friend. (For information on the various medical issues and risks associated with fasting, speak with your health care provider.)

4. Pray.

After you determine why you need to fast and what type of fast you'll do, the final step is to pray. Someone told me years ago that if you fast without praying, then you're just going hungry. Prayer is a key step to fasting.

If you're fasting in order to give God permission to deal with stubborn worry issues but need words for praying, then you can follow the acronym ACTS to pray specifically about this issue. I've also included some wording directed specifically at overcoming those stubborn worry issues, if you aren't sure what to say.

A for Adoration:

Dear God, You are the almighty God of the universe. You are all-powerful, all-knowing, and always present in every single circumstance of my life. God, You love me with an everlasting love, and I am so grateful that You sent Jesus to die for me.

C for Confession:

> God, You know that I've struggled with constant worry most every day. I hate that I can't stop worrying. God, I'm sorry for the times when I've chosen worry over prayer. But I don't want to live that way anymore.

T for Thanksgiving:

> I am so grateful that You provided _____ for me today. Thank You, God, for the people You've put in my life to love or to take care of me. I am especially grateful for
>
> _____.

S for Supplication:

> God, I am giving You permission to deal with whatever keeps causing worry to pop up in my life. Give my medical and mental health professionals the wisdom to identify and help me deal with anxiety issues that are affecting my physical and mental health. I also pray that while I fast, You will allow some of those deep-down worry strongholds to surface in my life so You can destroy them.

If you've decided that God is leading you toward a fast in order to deal with some deep-seated worry, but you aren't quite ready to give up food for an entire day, then a first step can be eliminating one meal and drinking water or broth instead.

Today's final thought on fasting as a secret weapon:
If I want God to get rid of my deep-down worry, then I need to focus time and effort on deep-down worship.

18

Four Ways to Ruin a Good Fight

The best advice in order to face each day is this: Hope for the best, get ready for the worst, and then take whatever God sends.

—Barbara Johnson, *The Best Devotions of Barbara Johnson*

*H*ave you ever gained back the weight you've lost? (Don't roll your eyes at me.)

After the birth of my first child, I joined a weight loss program and changed my life around so I could lose weight. Creating a routine around my new lifestyle habits was tough. Cutting and chopping vegetables took a lot more time than just sliding a tray of frozen fried chicken in the oven. I was still in college at the time, so managing a full-course load, a part-time job, a toddler, and a husband taxed my daily energy. But I had to find both energy and time to work out too. I didn't think I could keep up the new habits and routine. However, as I saw the weight drop, the momentum and excitement for my new routine increased.

I still remember reaching my goal weight the summer I graduated. I felt so proud not only that I'd lost weight but also that I had made good choices for my health even when I didn't feel like making them.

After I graduated from college, my new job required long hours, so I couldn't work out as often. As much as I knew that I was risking all of my hard work and success, I craved easy choices. What could be easier than McDonald's drive-thru across the street from my office or the Chinese carryout up the road? The more stress or worry I felt, the easier it was to slip back into old, comfortable behaviors, even if those behaviors were the cause of my dissatisfaction.

Recently, I went online to check out the *Biggest Loser: Where Are They Now?* updates to see who'd kept the weight off and who hadn't. My heart broke. Most of the contestants in that update had gained most, if not all, of their weight back. The show has been criticized for its methods, and researchers have actually studied why so many contestants had gained back the weight.[1] *Biggest Loser* former executive producer J. D. Roth decided to profile contestants in a new show to find out their stories of postshow weight gain. "They started the Biggest Loser unfit, unhealthy and unhappy. Then, they finished the Biggest Loser hopeful, skinny, fit, and ready to take on the world. But somewhere along the way, their old habits crept back in. And unfortunately, so did the pounds."[2]

The frustrating cycle of gaining and losing weight is a powerful and personal example that most of us can relate to. Even if your story is reversed and you've struggled with trying to gain weight and then losing it, you understand the frustration of fighting to change habits, finding success, and then watching it slip away.

As I mentioned near the start of our journey together, fighting your worry battle is never just about learning how to not freak out if your spouse is a few hours late coming home or if your car repair bill is $1,200 and you don't have the money. The point of learning how to fight in faith is to learn how to turn your worry into worshiping the God who is with us and for us in every circumstance, whether real or imagined.

What does it take for us to keep using what we've learned so we don't fall back into old habits and behaviors? We're going to look at the "Where Are They Now?" situation in Joshua's life. Several years had passed, and though we read about Joshua's incredible success against many mighty kings, the Israelites weren't experiencing the victory that God had promised. They'd stopped fighting and, as a result, no longer tasted the thrill of victory. It was time for God to have a frank conversation with Israel's valiant leader.

Losing Your Drive

Joshua 12 lists thirty-one kings that Joshua and the Israelites defeated in battle. Those kings represented the downfall of Canaan's top level of power and influence. After the kings were beaten, God commanded the Israelites to completely destroy the inhabitants of their newly conquered land.

You might be asking hard questions about why God would command the Israelites to extinguish the inhabitants of those lands and take possession. In fact, when skeptics read about the Israelites' conquest of the Promised Land, they accuse God of being ruthless, cold, and vengeful. You might even harbor that same opinion. A common question goes like this: *If God was so loving, then why did He order all of those people to die?* I love the words spoken by my pastor, Ben Snyder, when we have tough questions about Bible texts: "We all want simple answers to the most complex questions about God and life. Yet, God is not simple, and neither are we. One look at our genetic code alone reminds us that we are wonderfully complex. Perhaps God knows that the best way to give us answers is to invite us to seek Him" (Hebrews 11:6).

Since I don't want your worry battle to get sidetracked on this issue, perhaps this brief background information might help: There is a large historical context behind what we read in Joshua. The campaign to conquer the Promised Land was actually hundreds of years in the making.[3]

God actually gave the people in Canaan four hundred years to turn away from their sinful ways before sending the Israelites to conquer them. In Genesis 15:16, God made an agreement with Abraham as he stood in Canaan hundreds of years before Joshua and the Israelites entered the Promised Land. "After four generations your descendants will return here to this land, for the Amorites do not yet warrant their destruction."

This is an early foreshadow of grace for non-Israelites, similar to the invitation to salvation for non-Jews in the New Testament. The Amorites were given many generations to turn to God, and we saw evidence of this through Rahab and the Gibeonites' testimony. However, many more did not. What unfolds in the Book of Joshua is the culmination of events for both the blessing of the Israelites and the judgment of the Amorites.

As we come back to the present situation for the Israelites, the kings were defeated but the land had not been conquered. Those were two separate conquests. It was like killing a wasp, but leaving the hive as it is. As long as you don't deal with the hive, those wasps are going to keep coming.

By now Joshua was an old man. He had been the leader for a long time, and even though the Israelites were at rest from war (Joshua 11:23), the task that Joshua was given had not been finished. God told him, "You are growing old, and much land remains to be conquered" (13:1). Then God outlined an extensive list of territory that Joshua and the Israelites would need to fight in order to take possession of the land.

Imagine working for your company for fifty years and just as you begin dreaming about retirement, your boss tells you about all of the missed reports or overdue projects. If you don't work in the marketplace, imagine working diligently in your home for forty years and then someone opening a secret room filled with hundreds of loads of laundry. How tempting would it be to say, "Forget it!" or "I can live without it"?

If I had been Joshua, I might have been discouraged at the thought of having to rally the troops again after years of fighting. *God, those troops are finally settling into their new lives. I know that it's not all that You gave us, but we're good with this.* In our battle against worry, there can be a time when we experience some success and we're doing all right—until God shows us a place where we haven't finished our worry battle or a fresh new fight that needs to be fought. Once we realize how much energy and focus that fighting will require, motivation can be a real problem.

Then, God's words to Joshua at the end of that depressing status update hold an important tension. God said, "I myself will drive these people out of the land ahead of the Israelites" (Joshua 13:6). God's promise to drive out the inhabitants was conditional on this Israelites' obedience to following God's commands. Here's how one commentary writer explains it: "Each tribe was responsible to possess their own land completely. God is high on the concept of personal responsibility and initiative."[4]

We can feel that same tension when it comes to our worry battle. Yes, God will give us victory over worry, but we have to do our part. And we can't just do our part when we feel like it. If we want God's victory over worry, we've got to win our worry battle God's way.

What is it about us as Christians that we can experience moments of great spiritual victory, but then later we're willing to settle back into the way things used to be—as if God had never shown up in our lives? It's not God who suffers; it's us! Have you had those "on-fire" seasons with Jesus when it was you and God against the world? Months later, you're barely going to church and your Bible app hasn't opened in six months. What happened?

There are four attitudes that will wreck our battle against worry. We see these attitudes surface among the Israelites in Judges 1. That chapter is written like a "Where Are They Now?" update.

The events in Judges 1 took place after the death of Joshua. The Israelites still hadn't taken complete possession of the land God had given them, so they asked God which one of the twelve tribes should attack the Canaanites. God answered, "the tribe of Judah." So, the fighting men of Judah and the tribe of Simeon went to battle and defeated King Adoni-bezek's troops. The people of Judah had even more success against many other enemies, but then, they ran into trouble with the Canaanites, who owned iron chariots. They were unable to drive those people out.

If you're like me, you might be wondering, *Wait a minute! If God promised to give the Israelites victory over their enemies, then why didn't they experience that victory?* There are two questions that we must consider: Did God fail to keep His promise? Or, did the Israelites not follow through in faith on God's promise?

As we read the "Where Are They Now?" update in Judges 1, we can see four attitudes that I call "worry drivers" because when we experience them, they will always drive us back to worry.

- Weariness: the Israelites had gotten tired of fighting.
- Compromise: they had developed an affinity for the inhabitants.
- Apathy: they had stopped caring and decided to settle.
- Doubt: they had lost faith that they could win.

I can see myself in the Israelites' struggle. There have been times in my worry battle when each one of these four worry drivers picked me up and drove me back into the wide world of worry.

Which one of those worry drivers appears to be active in your life? If none are active, which one(s) must you guard against?

If you aren't sure which worry drivers might be active in your life, but you know that you aren't fighting in faith as you should, this is a great time to review chapter 8, "Circumcision of the Heart," and do the self-examination exercise again. That exercise is a wonderful monthly or quarterly temperature check that will clear out the spiritual shrapnel so that you'll be spiritually healthy and whole as you continue to fight in faith.

In between those temperature checks, how do we learn how to stay the course each day so that we can continue to walk in the victory that we've already received?

Keeping Your Drive

In John 16, Jesus was preparing His disciples for His arrest, crucifixion, and death. After many years of walking with them on earth, providing one-to-one teaching and spiritual direction, Jesus knew it was time to accomplish the purpose for which He had come to earth. In His final message to them, Jesus admonished them to walk in the truth that He'd taught them and to live empowered by the Holy Spirit. Then Jesus summarizes the "why" behind His address: "I have told you all this so that you may have peace in me. Here on earth you will have many trials and sorrows. But take heart, because I have overcome the world" (v. 33).

Jesus's words were not the kind of talk the disciples wanted to hear. I imagine that they wanted to shout, "But Jesus, You've done some really great stuff. We don't understand why it has to end this way. Can't You use the power that You used to feed five thousand people to get rid of our enemies? Then we can be happy and not have to deal with all of that stuff!"

As Jesus told them that the days to come would be marked by difficulty and persecution, I wonder if the disciples began watching their own mental movies of pain and hardship.

Knowing that His words might cause fear, Jesus was quick to remind them that victory has already been won. He has overcome! The original Greek word for "overcome" (or "conquered" in some translations) is *nikao*, meaning "carry off the victory from battle," from the word *nike*, which you might recognize as the name of the iconic athletic brand.[5] In this case, Jesus was speaking about victory, and He hadn't even gone to the cross at the time He spoke those words. Yet, His confidence came because He knew God's power. We can have the same confidence in God's power too. Now you can say the following every morning: "Since Jesus has already overcome, I will overcome, too!"

Perhaps you can write that statement down on a note card and tape it next to your bathroom mirror. I had a friend who used to write God's promises on note cards and hang them all over her bathroom. She struggled with having confidence in God's promises for her life. Merrie read those cards every morning while brushing her teeth. Within a year's time, those words had sunk so far into her heart and mind that they became a solid foundation for a strong faith. The same can happen for you!

What does being an overcomer mean? Unless you like living in unhappy despair, it means everything! When you wake up in the morning, you have already overcome whatever you're going to face during the day. You've overcome your worries over your annual performance review. You have overcome the fear of isolation. As God's son or daughter, you have access to God's power for your life, so you can break down the worry drivers by holding on to your overcomer mind-set.

Every day, you will fight some kind of worry battle because our lives are filled with uncertainty each day, both real and imagined. Even if you try to bubble wrap your life by living as a hermit on the side of a mountain, you can't completely eliminate uncertainty. You still can't know the future, even if you try to shrink down the possibilities of what could go wrong.

The worry battles that I fought five years ago are different from the worry battles I face now. If I'm being honest, I feel like I'm fighting harder battles now. Is that actually true? I don't know. Maybe the battles feel harder because I have to fight harder to not fall prey to one of the four worry drivers. Maybe the battles feel harder because I've trained for adversity, so smaller worries shut down quicker, but the king-sized worries drain my energy and effort. Either way, I don't have to keep my eyes on the obstacle that I'm facing because I can focus on Jesus, who has already overcome and given me victory in my situation. Then my focus can be on working toward my victory by staying in step with God, whether it's letting Him lead, applying a tool, or activating my secret weapon. All of these equip me to engage in battle as I'm waiting for the day when the battle is over and Jesus opens my eyes to see the final victory.

Today's final thought:
I am an overcomer, and my worry battle will not be undermined by unhealthy attitudes or behaviors.

189

19

Asking for God's Best

Never settle for less than God's best!

—Barb Roose

O
ne day in late December, I was sitting in the living room and thinking about returning to campus for the second half of my freshman year of college. Christmas break was almost over, and I didn't have enough money to pay for my books. I worried about how to stretch the little bit of money that I'd earned over break into the hundreds of dollars that I needed for books.

My dad walked in and sat down in the chair opposite of mine. He asked, "So, do you need book money?"

I froze and my eyes got big. I was terrified that if I admitted I didn't have book money, maybe my dad would tell me that I needed to stay home and work winter semester to save. I stayed silent because I didn't want to lie to my father.

Dad sat down on the couch next to me. He opened his wallet and pulled out a hundred-dollar bill. He put it on the coffee table and asked, "Is this enough?"

Again, I didn't know what to say. Was this a trick?

Dad pulled out another hundred-dollar bill and laid it next to the first one. "Is this enough?"

By this point, tears began rolling down my face. I just stared at the money. I'd been stressing out late at night and jittery during the day because I didn't know where the money would come from, and there it was, lying a foot away from me.

Dad pulled out one more hundred-dollar bill and placed it next to the other bills. He asked one more time, "Is this enough?"

I nodded my head.

He picked up the bills and handed me the money. Then he sat back on the couch and waited until I looked him in the eye. All he said was, "Why didn't you ask for the book money?"

I didn't ask Mom and Dad because I felt guilty about asking for help. College was expensive, and my brother and sister were still living at home, so I'd made up my mind that they couldn't, or they wouldn't, or they shouldn't help me.

My one-sided judgment created a lot of stress and worry in my life. Wouldn't it have been better for me to ask them when my need arose? I could have saved myself a Christmas break's worth of sleepless nights. If they couldn't have helped me, then at least they would have been aware of the problem and we would have come up with other solutions together, instead of me bearing the entire weight on my own.

Would you rather seek out a blessing or bear the burden? My friend and leadership consultant, Michael Daughinee, likes to say, "Healthy people ask for what they want, even if they don't get it." His words ring in my ears on a regular basis because my default setting is to try to work whatever I want on my own. Yet, there is a blind spot in my life where I'm wholly and totally unaware of the millions of ways that God has blessed me without my knowledge or comprehension.

If you tend to suffer under your burden because you're afraid to ask God for a blessing, I hope the words in James 4:2-3 change your perspective: "You don't have what you want because you don't ask God for it. And even when you ask, you don't get it because your motives are all wrong—you want only what will give you pleasure." Sometimes I'll say no to God's help. I'll think about asking God for something, but then I'll think, *Nah. God doesn't need to do that for me.* Then I'll stress myself out by trying to take care of the need myself. I believe that when I get to heaven, God will show me all the blessings that He wanted to give me, but I was too afraid to ask.

Do you struggle to ask God for help or even a blessing? When we look in the pages of Scripture, especially in the stories of two people we're going to learn about in this chapter, we can see that God loves to give His children gifts. While God's not a divine vending machine and doesn't make deals, God is generous, and He loves to be generous toward us.

Standing in Line for a Blessing

One day, a man named Caleb came to see Joshua. It had been many years since the kings were defeated, but the Israelites still had a lot of land to be divided among the tribes. This land was an inheritance for the tribes and was the fulfillment of a promise that God had made to Abraham hundreds of years before. Each tribe was to receive an inheritance from God, but many years before, God had instructed Moses, in addition, to promise inheritances to a few individuals. Caleb was one of those individuals.

Many years before, Joshua and Caleb had been part of the group of twelve spies that Moses sent to spy on the Promised Land. When the spies came back, ten of the spies were worried about getting killed by the giants in the land. Joshua and Caleb were the only two who tried to encourage the people to believe God's promises for victory. In the end, the people rebelled against God, and their punishment was to remain in the wilderness for forty years, until the rebellious adults died off. The only two people who would survive the rebellion would be Caleb and Joshua. Decades had passed since that day in the desert. Now Caleb had come back to Joshua. I can see Caleb standing before the only other man to survive the wilderness for forty years. I imagine the men looking each other eye to eye. While there's no record of how often they saw each other in the years since arriving in Canaan, there's no doubt that their shared history still played loudly in their memories.

Both men had known what it was like to see the Promised Land before anyone else, including Moses. Both men had known what it was like to watch an entire assembly of people rise up and threaten to kill them. Both men had watched as one by one, every adult they knew died in the wilderness.

Now, an eighty-five-year-old Caleb presented himself to Joshua to claim a personal inheritance that Moses had assigned to him long ago. Usually, by Caleb's age, an individual is *giving* an inheritance, not accepting one. However, Caleb wasn't worried about his age. He said, "I am as strong now as I was when Moses sent me on that journey, and I can still travel and fight as well as I could then…If the Lord is with me, I will drive them out of the land, just as the Lord said" (Joshua 14:11-12).

In my mind, Caleb looks like an aged version of Rocky Balboa. A little wrinkly, but still fit, with the heart of a fighter. It's not hard to imagine this buff-looking, barrel-chested grandpa standing tall with his head held high and a gleam in his eye. With that kind of vitality, I would be surprised if Caleb wasn't out there when the Israelites conquered Jericho or defeated the soldiers at Ai. If he could still travel and fight, that meant that he was still traveling and fighting on a regular basis.

Don't you want to be like Caleb if God allows you to live until you're eighty-five? There are a few ladies in my life around that age, and these brave, bold sisters cast a vision for who I want to be years from now. Like Caleb, these women have fought in faith over the years, battling not only worry but also the personal heartache that touches each one of our lives. These women are warriors of the faith, and I want to grow up to be just like them. I want to be able to say that I've held on to my strength and I could still take on whatever opportunities God sent my way.

Blessings aren't turnkey; they often require sacrifice or responsibility. If God blesses you with a house, you've still got to maintain it and protect it. If God blesses you with a child or a marriage, you've got to invest in those relationships and sacrifice for them.

Caleb's inheritance would also need some work. He had to go in and fight for it. He knew that some of those inhabitants were actually giants, descendants of Anak, and he was ready to fight them too. This is such a contrast to the last chapter when, even years later, most of the Israelite tribes had failed to drive out the inhabitants.

After receiving his inheritance, Caleb went right to work and drove out the giants living on the land. Even as Caleb gives us a great illustration of boldness, we also learn this lesson from his daughter, Aksah. Whenever I see her name, I think "Ask-ah" because, even after she'd already received, she asked her father for even more: "Give me another gift. You have already given me land in Negev; now please give me springs of water, too." (Joshua 15:19).

Raise your hand if Aksah's request sounds greedy. *Give me another gift.* She came right out and asked for a freebie. She didn't beat around the bush or try to bargain. Aksah just asked the big ask. I admire that, even if it makes me uncomfortable because I'm often not that bold. What if Aksah's request was to help her husband support the needs of their household? Caleb had the resources to give, and if the request was made to help build for the future, then why shouldn't she ask?

How did her father answer? "So Caleb gave her the upper and lower springs." Aksah asked for springs of water, and she received two springs. *You have not because you ask not . . .*

Jesus's message in Matthew 7:11 was such a big one that he repeated it in Luke 11. Here's Matthew's rendering: "So if you sinful people know who to give good gifts to your children, how much more will your heavenly Father give good gifts to those who ask him." God only knows how to give good gifts to His children. Yet, if you are in the midst of a tragic or painful life circumstance that is keeping you awake at night, that doesn't feel so good. However, God's goodness isn't about a small window of time, and it's much bigger than our perspective. God sees and knows your pain, but He's also saying to you, "Don't you worry, My beloved child. Wait until you see what I've got for you."

Settling for Less than God's Best

There is a sad, hot-mess story that you might miss if you're just skimming through the Book of Joshua. But when we're talking about settling for less than God's best, this is the story that must be told.

While there were twelve tribes of Israel, not every tribe received the same type of land allotment. One of those tribes ran into trouble claiming their land: "As for the tribe of Dan, the Amorites forced them back into the hill country and would not let them come down into the plains" (Judges 1:34).

That could not have been an easy situation for the people of Dan. Not only did they get trounced, but living in the mountains wouldn't be easy. Imagine trying to grow anything, build homes, or raise animals. So, why didn't they come back and fight again? After all, God had renewed His promise to Joshua to drive out the inhabitants so that the Israelites could claim their inheritance.

When we follow the tribe of Dan's story into the future, we discover that not only did they abandon God's instructions for fighting to remove the Amorites, but they ended up settling for far less than God wanted to give them.

Eventually, the people of Dan decide that they wanted to find a place to live outside of the mountains. By this time, Joshua had died and there wasn't a new leader for the Israelites. Without a leader, the people were not living according to their covenant with God, so all kinds of abominable religious practices were commonplace.

A group of five Danites began scouting, looking for a new home. They ended up at the house of an Israelite man named Micah. After he stole eleven hundred pieces of silver from his mother and returned it, she used two hundred of those pieces to create silver idols for their home, which is the complete opposite of how God called them to live. Then an unnamed wandering Levite showed up at Micah's home. Since the Levites were responsible for the religious life among the Israelites, Micah hired the young man as a rent-a-priest for ten pieces of Mom's silver per year.

When the five Danite men showed up, they asked the Levite to consult with God about their mission to find a new inheritance because the first one that God gave them didn't work out.

Already this story feels like a mess. A hot mess is what happens when people blaze a trail for their lives without God. And then it gets worse.

The five Danite men scouted the city of Laish, the northernmost city in the Promised Land, and very far away from their original land inheritance. The Danites saw that the people of Laish were prosperous and quiet, so the city felt like a good target. When the scouts returned home, they reported that the fighting men should attack.

The tribe of Dan was about to trade their spacious land allotment for a single city far away from where God assigned them. Not only that, but the Danites liked the fact that the people of Laish were quiet and unassuming. Seems like they wanted an easier target since the Amorites had whooped up on them before.

On their way to Laish, the six hundred fighting men of Dan

stopped by Micah's house and the five Danite men who'd been there before went in and stole several items, including the silver idols. When the priest confronted them, they told him to put a hand over his mouth and come with them.

After a brief showdown with an unhappy Micah, the Danite soldiers invaded Laish, killing everyone and razing the city. When they rebuilt it, they named the city Dan.

There are many reasons to be heartbroken while reading this story. First, the people of Dan not only rejected their inheritance from God but also didn't believe His promise by which to claim their inheritance. They stopped fighting. Second, they settled for a fraction of what God had promised them. They compromised. When you look at the map and see the one little city, it looks so sad compared to what they didn't fight for years before. Finally, they didn't even know what they were missing out on. They cheated themselves. That's the most heartbreaking part of it all.

This is one of the most challenging stories for me because deep inside, I know there are times when I'm missing out on what God wants to give me. He's already given me so much, but that doesn't mean He doesn't want to give me more. However, I get in my own way sometimes by either saying no before I even ask God or settling for less than God's best for my life.

How can you know if you're settling for less than God's best? There are three lessons we can take from the Danites' story that will answer that question:

1. You've stopped fighting for what God has already given you.
2. You've compromised yourself for someone or something that God doesn't want you to have.
3. You have no idea what God wants to give you in the first place.

Take a moment and consider where you may have settled for less than God's promised best in your life. If there are places where you've neglected to let God lead or failed to consult Him before making a decision, it's not too late to stop and pray:

> God, I never want to settle for less than Your best for my life. I want to bring _____ before You right now. God, I'm quieting my heart and mind to listen for You to speak, and I will respond in obedience to whatever You are calling me to do, whether it's to step out in faith toward one of Your promises or to let go of pursuing something or someone that's less than Your best for me. Thank You for wanting what's best for me in every area of life. Amen.

Fighting for God's Best

There was one group of women whose story contrasts greatly with the pitiful story of the Danites. These women are known as the daughters of Zelophehad, and they are introduced for the first time in Numbers 26:33: "One of Hepher's descendants, Zelophehad, had no sons, but his daughters were Mahlah, Noah, Hoglah, Milcah and Tirzah."

There's no mention that these women had husbands or sons, so they knew that when land was handed out to the individual families, they would be left without provision. Quite simply, women didn't inherit land; they received dowries when they married. Land was for sons to receive from their father's estate at death.

I love how these women appeared before Moses, the priest, the leaders of their tribe, and the entire Israelite community. Now, that's super brave! In her *Make Your Move* Bible study, Lynn Cowell shares the story of the Zelophehad sisters, whom she affectionately calls "the daughters of Z." She paints a picture of the questions that the women might have faced as they stood before the Israelite community. "*No one has ever done this before. Who do we think we are? What will the leaders think of us? Will the women of our community think we're too bold? What if the panel of men say no?"* Then, Lynn poses a challenging thought that many of us have grappled with: "Culture constantly makes us aware of 'our place' and challenges whether we have what it takes."[1]

While I wasn't there, I could see those women standing together, side by side. If they were bold enough to walk up there in front of that crowd, then I'm going to believe that when they opened their mouths to speak, they addressed the crowd with confidence.

When Moses went before God to consult Him about the five sisters' request, God answered, "The claim of the daughters of Zelophehad is legitimate. You must give a grant of land with their father's relatives. Assign them the property that would have been given to their father" (Numbers 27:7). Then God changed the future by declaring that if a man has no sons, his inheritance should go to his daughter, not the next nearest male relative.

In Joshua 17, the daughters of Zelophehad presented themselves before Joshua to claim their land grant. They may have waited many years, so those women did not settle for less than God's best for their lives.

In a day and age when people are chasing material excess, let's make it our goal to receive God's best. The good news is that as God's children, we are His heirs. As John Piper says, "If you are an heir of God, then you will inherit what is God's."[2] If we think about what God has, it's everything that we could possibly want! Not just the fact that God is sovereign over all the heavens and earth, but we also are heirs to God's character and power. Everything that God is, He gives to us! Let me ask you a question: Would you rather experience life infused with God's character and power or life on your own?

⌒☉ℛℴ⌒

A final thought:
God cares about each area of your life, and His best is the very best for you.

❧ 20 ❧

Carefrontations

Instruct the wise, and they will be even wiser.
Teach the righteous, and they will learn even more.

—Proverbs 9:9

*I*n 2015, award-winning singer Mandisa was in a deep and dangerous depression. Her best friend, Kisha Mitchell, had passed away in 2014 while pregnant and battling breast cancer. Not only did Mandisa retreat from her friends and from making music, but she gained almost two hundred pounds in the process. One night, Mandisa left home to go to the movies, and when she came back to her car, there were notes taped all over her car from concerned friends. The notes had handwritten messages expressing their love and concern for her. They were waiting for her and staged an intervention. "They insisted that I get counseling, and that is what helped me finally start dealing with my grief. If that hadn't happened, I probably wouldn't be here today."[1] Mandisa followed through with getting counseling, and she's back to making music again and taking care of herself.

Notice how she credits those friends who stepped up and stepped into her life with love and truth with putting her back on the path toward God's purpose for her life. I'm sure it wasn't easy for those friends, who knew she could have been offended or even blocked them from her life even longer. Yet, they took a courageous step to speak truth into her life. Have you ever been worried about someone and tried to tell that loved one about your concerns? Perhaps you have a spouse who works too much or an adult child who's in an unhealthy relationship. For many of us, just the thought of speaking up about issues can make us feel nervous, uncomfortable, and anxious. We don't want to risk hurting the person or messing up our relationship. Some of you grew up in homes where *confrontation* was a bad word; therefore, as an adult, you avoid confrontation like a dirty diaper on a hot day. Trisha Yearwood can relate. She said, "My upbringing did not create a healthy affection for confrontation. I'd love it if everyone always got along and nothing ever got tense."[2]

In chapter 14, "Secondhand Worry," you learned how to avoid taking on other people's worries. Now you're going to learn some lessons about how to step up and step into difficult conversations with people you care about but who are engaged in behaviors that aren't good for them.

Mandisa's friends staged what psychotherapist Harris Stratyner calls a "carefrontation." Dr. Stratyner created the treatment approach to help addicted individuals, who often got defensive or shut down during confrontation. According to Dr. Stratyner, a carefrontation approach allows for a kinder, gentler road toward accountability and treatment.

For years, my church staff friends and I have used the term *carefrontation.* If you're a church staffer or pastor's wife, you know that there are times when it feels like all you do is have hard conversations with people. We joked about that term because it was a bit of a corny yet powerful reminder to begin every difficult conversation with lots of love and care before clearly expressing the truth.

As I mentioned, life in ministry is filled with difficult conversations. Sometimes I was the target of those conversations.

During a speaking engagement a few seasons back, I was tired. Normally, I'm a fountain of energy, but I had been rushing that day due to extra meetings and driving. I prayed for extra strength and powered through the evening. While I had a smile on my face, I was counting down the hours until I could return home and climb into bed.

It seems that I wasn't as good of an actress as I thought. A good friend noticed my weariness and sent me a message the next day because she was concerned about my physical health and spiritual well-being.

We talked on the phone that afternoon. She asked questions about my schedule, rest periods, and stress levels. Then she inquired about my spiritual health and family relationships. Some of the questions were tough, and rather than accept simple answers, she pressed in a little deeper.

As I answered my friend honestly about taking on too many extra commitments in a short period of time, I began to see into that blind spot. Ouch.

When I hung up the phone, I felt a little raw. It's hard allowing someone to point out yellow-light or red-light issues in my life. I like feeling good about myself, so confronting the truth about my less-than-awesomeness is tough. Yet, I cherish that conversation because God sent someone to my life to illuminate a dark place that didn't align with God's best for my life. Since I want God's best, I need people in my life to help me stay on track toward it.

There are times in life when we see the people we love sliding off track, whether due to bad people who've hurt them, bad news that derails them, or bad decisions that consume them. In those situations, we need a plan to lovingly address them and pray for God to intervene in their lives.

Before we talk about what this kind of conversation looks like and why it's important, we're going to look into a situation where the Israelites on the western side of the Jordan responded to a questionable situation happening with the Israelite tribes on the eastern side.

Watching Out for Each Other

After many years, it was now time for the fighting men from the eastern tribes of Reuben, Gad, and East Manasseh to return home to their wives and families on the other side of the river. See, when Moses gave permission for those tribes to settle, he made the fighting men in those tribes promise that they would stay and fight with the western tribes until the land was conquered. If they didn't, then the tribes would lose their inheritance.

Now that the fighting was over, the men of the eastern tribes began the journey home. On their way home, they stopped near the Jordan River on the west side and constructed a large altar.

We'll discover their motives for constructing the altar in just a bit, but it's clear that news of this altar was very disturbing for the western Israelites, who are ready to make war. Joshua had just reminded the eastern tribes to follow and serve God alone (Joshua 22:5), and now the eastern tribes had built an altar—presumably, they thought, to a false god—without Joshua's knowledge or approval. The Israelites met to make war against the eastern tribes. They meant business!

But then, instead, a delegation, including a member of the high priest's family and leaders from each tribe of Israel, set off to investigate. I applaud the western tribes for going to find out what was going on. Rather than just wishing the departing tribes adios and good luck, the people of Israel recognize that while the Jordan River may have split them geographically, they were one spiritually as a people.

When the delegation arrived, they immediately began asking questions. They essentially say, "Are you crazy? Don't you remember the thousands of people who died in the plague at Peor? Have you forgotten about Achan being stoned? Don't do this to us!"

The leader of the delegation was a priest named Phinehas, whose zeal for upholding God's righteousness is recorded in Numbers 25.

Earlier in Israel's history, while the entire assembly were camped at Peor, the Israelite men had been seduced by idol-worshiping Canaanite women. Not only that, but they had gone off with those women to offer sacrifices to the god Baal. As a result of their sin, a great plague began killing thousands of people.

During the plague, God ordered Moses to round up all the men who had participated in idol worship so that they could be killed. Immediately the plague stopped when Phinehas, who had a heart for holiness and purity, killed an Israelite man and the Canaanite woman he had taken back to his tent—an act of defiant sin against God. Phinehas rushed in on the passionate couple and killed them both with one thrust of a spear. God's anger and the plague then ended because of Phinehas's actions.

With this background in mind, as I read the words of the delegation here in Joshua 22, I can imagine the intensity in Phinehas's eyes as he, and perhaps other leaders of the delegation, fired off questions and a quick history recap for the eastern tribes. They had seen the sin of individuals affect the entire community before, and they did not want a repeat incident.

Once Phinehas and the rest of the delegation realized that the altar, named "Witness," had been built to serve as a witness that the eastern and western tribes worshiped the same Lord (Joshua 22:34), the matter was settled. I admire the integrity and courage of the delegation. I know from experience that when there is uncertainty in a matter, it takes a lot of bravery to approach another believer and, in love and respect, question the veracity of that individual's faith. I've been on both sides, and it's hard. Yet this is exactly what God calls us to do.

How are we supposed to model the wisdom of the Israelites in today's time? The teachings of the New Testament direct Christians to confront other Christians about sinful behavior. As brothers and sisters in Christ, we are all part of God's family together. If our desire is to live for Christ, then it makes sense that we'd pull one another up if a sin issue pulls us down. Galatians 6:1 tell us, "If another believer is overcome by some sin, you who are godly should gently and humbly help that person back onto the right path. And be careful not to fall into the same temptation yourself."

Notice how the writer's instructions not only include what to do but also how to do it. When we sit down with a believer caught up in sin, we're not supposed to beat him with our Bibles or berate him for his struggle. Unfortunately, many of us have been singed and scarred by the caustic words of other Christians who thought that they were on a mission for God when they criticized or condemned us.

We're to "gently and humbly" help those who have fallen. This means that we're to not see ourselves as any better than them, and our words should include a generous scoop of truth and love. The way I see it, God is the originator of the carefrontation concept, and it's time more Christians learned how to do confrontation His way!

In Matthew 18, Jesus provided a crucial and helpful framework for confrontation that would prevent a lot of the trauma and drama in our churches. He addresses His disciples and begins with the first step, "If another believer sins against you, go privately and point out the offense" (v. 15).

Let's stop right there. I want to make sure that you were paying attention to Jesus's teaching because He gave one key piece of instruction that we're missing these days in the church. Jesus said, "Go privately." What does that mean? It means to go right to the person and talk with him or her instead of putting the conversation on blast for everyone to dip their ears and opinions in it.

If the other person claims to follow Christ, then he or she should be thinking about Paul's words in Colossians 3:12: "You must clothe yourselves with tenderhearted mercy, kindness, humility, gentleness and patience." If both individuals approach the conversation with these words in mind, then the situation can be aired openly and honestly, and the path to forgiveness and reconciliation can begin.

Jesus continued His teaching: "If the other person listens and confesses, you have won that person back" (Matthew 18:15). The operative word is "if." When someone doesn't want to listen, you can't make her. You've got to let it go and ask God to speak into her heart.

Jesus continued to teach in Matthew 18 about what to do if the first conversation isn't successful. During the second conversation, one or two witnesses should be present. Choosing individuals who clothe themselves with the same qualities in Colossians 3:12 is key. You don't want to ask a friend to come along who is a hothead. That's asking for trouble.

If you take a couple of witnesses and "the person refuses to listen," Jesus said, "take your case to the church." There are some high-level conflicts that require action at the highest level. At the point when the senior leaders of the church are involved, it's an important time to pray for God's wisdom in that situation.

At our church, our founding pastor, Lee, instructed our staff to ask people to follow the Matthew 18 principle before we'd schedule a meeting to get involved in the situation. If you're on staff at your church, how many phone calls and meetings take place because people can't or won't follow through on the first step of Jesus's Matthew 18 teaching? We can't be in such a hurry to play God and fix people's lives that we prevent them from this necessary step of discipleship.

What about confronting people caught in questionable, hurtful, or sinful behaviors who aren't Christians? There are times in life when we will need to talk with people whose destructive patterns cause harm to themselves and others. However, beating them over the head with a bunch of Bible verses won't be effective because they don't have the Holy Spirit working in their lives. Yet, God can use how you handle that conversation as a bridge for the gospel. Practically speaking, the carefrontation tool that follows will be helpful in your conversations with both Christians and non-Christians.

Carefrontation Sandwich Tool

Leila loves her mother, Sandra, but hates it when her mother calls to ask for money. Leila's parents divorced years ago, and Sandra raised Leila on her own. Five years ago, Sandra battled cancer but hasn't been able to return to work. Her disability payments are enough to cover her living expenses, but she overdrafts her account each month because she loves going out to lunch and shopping. Leila doesn't mind sending her mom a little money every now and then, but now, Sandra's calls are coming in every month, and the amount of money requested keeps growing. Now Leila dreads seeing her mom's number pop up on the screen. She knows that she needs to talk to her mom, and she feels bad because her mom's been through so much, but she is tired of the constant requests for money.

If you have a situation like Leila's and you aren't sure how to handle it, I want to introduce the carefrontation sandwich tool. This tool can be applied to behavioral issues, hurt feelings, and especially when you suspect that someone's life is sliding sideways into sin.

How do we proceed with a carefrontation? Since I like food, the best way for me to think about a carefrontation conversation is like a basic sandwich, which includes a slice of bread, meat, and another slice of bread. So, we're going to break this down and add in language that Leila could use in talking with her mother.

Step 1: A Slice of Love
Affirm the person's value and the relationship:

> Mom, you know how much I love you. I wouldn't have been able to make it through college without your love and support. I'm so grateful for you!

Step 2: Meat of Concern
Express observations, not opinions:

> I wonder if you knew that you've called me for six months in a row for extra money to cover your bills. I want you to be okay, but I am unable to afford to send money every month.

Step 3: Slice of Encouragement
Communicate goodwill and share hope for the future:

> My hope is that you have a chance to go over your monthly expenses to see where you can make things better. I know that you have enough to live on, and I'll be praying that God gives you wisdom and provision to live well.

As you can see, the carefrontation conversation is designed to be short and sweet. The more words we use, the higher the likelihood of causing confusion. It's also short because no one wants to sit through a long lecture. When I teach this method to my coaching clients, I tell them that the conversation should be fewer than two minutes long. After you finish speaking, your next move is to be silent and listen, if the other person has something to say. A carefrontation stops being caring if you argue or disagree with how the person feels. Even if you are right in the situation, remember that the relationship with the person matters more. Instead of engaging in verbal combat, consider the following replies: "Can you tell me more?" and "Thank you for sharing; let me think about that." End the conversation by letting your loved one know that you care and will continue to pray for him or her. Then pray!

One client used this method to "carefront" an adult child who was engaged in questionable online activity that could jeopardize a future job. When the client came in for the first appointment, she was upset and needed to talk her feelings out. I suggest that you do that too. A carefrontation isn't a time to process through all of your feelings. That's what a friend, counselor, or coach is there to do with you.

Once my client talked through her feelings, we rehearsed her carefrontation conversation. Why did we rehearse? Because our bodies don't like the feelings associated with confrontation, so when we rehearse, we help our minds and bodies practice for success. Even though the adult child lived far away, my client was able to use this tool to share her concerns, and to keep the lines of communication open in the relationship.

If you are thinking of someone you need to approach with a carefrontation, I believe this tool can help you. Take some time to pray and ask God about whether or not you should move forward with the carefrontation, then practice before you launch into that important conversation.

One final thought:
When we love others, we tell them the truth, and we do it with kindness and respect.

⊰ 21 ⊱

Even If . . .

Life is amazing. And then it's awful. And then it's amazing again.
And in between the amazing and the awful it's ordinary and
mundane and routine. Breathe in the amazing, hold on through the
awful, and relax and exhale during the ordinary. That's just living
heartbreaking, soul-healing, amazing, awful, ordinary life. And it's
breathtakingly beautiful.

—L. R. Knost, *Inhumanity*

'm starting this chapter in the waiting room of the palliative
care oncology unit of Summa Health Hospital in Akron,
Ohio. When I brainstormed this chapter weeks ago, I never
could have imagined that I'd be typing in this small room, listening to
the constant buzz of an automatic coffeemaker as I grapple with my
once-vibrant and strong father's end-of-life journey.

My sixty-seven-year-old dad was diagnosed with metastatic lung
cancer that had already spread to his liver and stomach. Dad's cancer
is advanced, and he's unable to tolerate treatment. At this moment,
our heads are spinning because everything is moving fast and we can't
catch up. He'd complained about a stomachache about five weeks
before. Within three weeks, he'd lost forty pounds off his muscular
frame. Dad's biopsy happened within a week of the first medical tests.

On the day that I'm writing this, we're preparing to meet with the hospice team. Wrapping my mind around Dad's rapidly unfolding cancer journey feels bewildering. According to what we know, his life will likely end before we have his full biopsy results. To know that at some point in the future we will experience the great pain of loss makes me want to run away and hide.

I don't want to go through this.

For those who've faced unexpected bad news followed by an uncertain future, you know that this kind of living feels like suffering whiplash before getting sucked up into a tornado.

This event in our lives means that I've had to grapple afresh with every concept and use every tool I've been writing about in this book. I've matched every worry with a prayer instead of beating myself up. I've killed a few eight-legged worries running around in my mind with meditating on God's Word. I'm intentionally building my mental train with God's promises and running that train from morning till night. I may not know what will happen in the future, but I know this: I don't want worry to steal even one second that I have left with my dad.

I know that great pain and loss are coming. How do we handle life when we're facing an uncertain but painful road? When the doctors say there is nothing else they can do or when the unwanted divorce papers are filed?

What does fighting in faith look like when our lives move from "what if" to "even if"? "Even if" captures the posture that even when heartache and hardship move into our lives, we can still choose to walk in God's victory.

Choices

Near the end of Joshua's life, he called the Israelites together one final time. Pretend that you are Joshua as he stands before the vast group that walked for more than fourteen thousand days in the desert and crossed the dry Jordan riverbed. His eyes had watched the walls of Jericho tumble down. The voice that addressed the people was the same voice that had called out to God to make the sun stand still for the day. We don't know how Joshua felt, but the fact that he had completed his God-given mission speaks volume to his leadership and faithfulness. The crowd knew that this would be Joshua's final address.

It's been awhile since we've seen our Israelite sister. We met her on the eastern side of the Jordan River, trying to listen to Moses while corralling her little children. Many years later, our friend has settled into her new home and managed the details of everyday life. Even as the fighting men were away for many years, battling for the very ground that she stood upon, our friend fought as well to establish a new life, which wasn't easy when starting all over again.

You know how, after you move, there's a rush to arrange the kitchen, unpack all the boxes, and set up the beds? You want to paint the walls, replace the flooring, and tear out the old landscaping as soon as possible. We feel that internal tension to toss out the old and establish the new normal so life can begin moving forward again.

Still, before the Israelites put all of the years of wandering in the desert and the fighting behind them, Joshua wanted to gather everyone together one more time. They'd reached a milestone moment. Almost five hundred years of history were coming to a close. Joshua wanted the Israelites to recognize their place in history and to use it to establish a firm foundation of faith for the future. To do that, Joshua created tension by challenging the Israelites with a choice.

As Joshua spoke to the people, he reminded them of God's mighty acts. Then Joshua looked upon the covenant community, a group of people who made a collective promise to serve God, and Joshua set the tension of individual choice:

So fear the Lord and serve him wholeheartedly. Put away forever the idols your ancestors worshiped when they lived beyond the Euphrates River and in Egypt. Serve the Lord alone. But if you refuse to serve the Lord, then choose today whom you will serve. Would you prefer the gods your ancestors served beyond the Euphrates? Or will it be the gods of the Amorites in whose land you now live? But as for me and my family, we will serve the Lord. (Joshua 24:14-15)

The iconic phrase, "choose today whom you will serve" is a popular sound bite that I've seen hanging on the front doors and foyers of many Christian homes. However, Joshua wasn't really giving the people a choice between God and other gods. Read carefully: Joshua implored the people to serve God wholeheartedly and abandon worshiping other idols. He called them to serve God only. Yet, they weren't being forced. They had a choice. If they did not want to serve God, Joshua told them to take their pick of the gods they would serve. It's in this moment that I imagine Joshua used a little sarcasm in his tone:

My fellow Israelites, you've seen all that God has done for you, but if you don't want to serve Him, you've got a few other choices. Do you want to pick the unknown gods in Mesopotamia, where our forefather Abraham was born? Remember, God rescued him from those gods so Abraham could be blessed by the true, almighty God. But, hey, if you want to go back to those gods, it's your choice. Or, do you want to serve the god of the Amorites, that our God trounced in battle? Friends, our mighty God has kicked their puny gods' butts. But, if you want to get cozy with those losers, go ahead. Like the song says, "It's your thang. Do what you want to do."

If the Israelites had already made a covenant agreement to serve God, then why was Joshua giving them a choice?

It's because God always gives us a choice, even if we don't choose Him.

Our American culture loves choice. Take jeans, for example. We can only wear one pair of jeans at a time, but that doesn't stop us from owning a collection of skinny, bootcut, low-rise, mid-rise, dark denim, light wash, or boyfriend styles. We like knowing that we've got options when we wake up in the morning, depending on how we feel. Yet even then, how many of us stand in our closets each morning in frustration, saying, "I don't know what to wear!"?

Choice always feels like it's liberating until it suffocates us or sets us on the wrong path. As the old proverb says, "There is a path before each person that seems right, but it ends in death" (Proverbs 14:12; 16:25). While there's a low chance that your outfit choice for today will be fatal, you can definitely kill your relationships, career, health, and self-esteem if you choose to follow the wrong authority in your life.

Joshua gave the people a choice because God did. But at the end of his monologue, Joshua told the people what his choice would be: "But as for me and my family, we will serve the Lord" (Joshua 24:15). Joshua's life wasn't perfect. He had made some mistakes and missteps, yet he knew that ups and downs with God on his side would be preferable to ups and downs without God.

Joshua wanted the Israelites to make a choice that would endure beyond how they felt or what was happening in their lives. "Even if" would eventually come into each of their lives. Not only would the Canaanites still be living among them, causing hardship in the future, but they would also experience the heartache that comes from existing in a sinful world.

Like the Israelites, every morning you wake up and God gives you a choice. You can read your Bible, or not. You can meditate on Scripture, or not. You can be obedient to God's Word or leading, or not. All of these choices are for you to make, and no one can force you to do otherwise. But "even if" is coming. And when it comes, you know that the first words out of your mouth will be, "O God!" So, choose to lean toward God today in order to prepare for whatever may come into your life tomorrow. Choosing God in advance of the "even if" is our best choice in preparing for heartache and hardship in the future.

After Joshua gave the people that final choice, they responded with:

> We would never abandon the Lord and serve other gods. For the Lord our God is the one who rescued us and our ancestors from slavery in the land of Egypt. He performed mighty miracles before our very eyes. As we traveled through the wilderness among our enemies, he preserved us. It was the Lord who drove out the Amorites and the other nations living here in the land. So we, too, will serve the Lord, for he alone is our God. (Joshua 24:16-18)

Their words sound good, don't they? But Joshua knew the wishy-washy track record of God's people. Their response reminds me of when my kids were in elementary school and they asked us for a dog. I'd say, "Who's going to take care of the dog when it's no longer a cute puppy?" My kids would respond, "We will! We promise!" We didn't believe them because we knew that over time, our kids' attention would drift from taking care of that dog to other things. That's human nature, to drift from our commitments toward compromise.

How many of us began the Christian life on fire for Jesus? We were excited about reading our Bibles, going to church, and praying. After a few months or years pass, we don't feel like going to church, or the pastor's messages don't seem to hit the spot anymore. Then we begin looking around for other people, places, or things to satisfy us.

As a rebuttal to the people's words, Joshua gave them a reality check. He intentionally brought the Israelites to a town called Shechem, the place where their forefather, Jacob (later Israel), buried the idols that his wife Rachel had stolen from her father's house when they fled from him. Joshua knew the story of Jacob and the idols, and that there were people in that community still worshiping idols even as their lips told a different story. As their mouths were saying yes to God, their lives were screaming no.

Where are the places that your life is saying no to God today? Those are the weak places that will crack and break apart when stress shows up in our lives. These are the thin fault lines that won't be able to stand up to the pressure of pain.

Yet, we can strengthen those places a little each day when we choose God. Every time we activate our choice to love God and love others, those choices have an exponential impact on strengthening us for the future. Memorizing a Bible verse isn't just about remembering some words. In the future, God will use that verse to give you hope, prevent you from making a bad decision, or give you the courage to leap forward.

When it comes to your worry battle, you also have a choice. At the end of this chapter, there's a covenant agreement that you can hold on to, to help you remember the choice that you've made each day.

Even If . . .

Long after Joshua died, the Israelites fell into centuries of a repetitive cycle of sin, punishment, rescue, and blessing. As much as we'd like to think that they learned a lesson after each round of punishment, a new generation would show up and repeat the mistakes of the past.

During one of those times, many years into the future, the prophet Habakkuk wrote of coming destruction. He knew that great heartache and pain would descend upon God's people. In the following verses, he cast a vision for a world where there was no food, and desolation was all around.

> Even though the fig trees have no blossoms,
> and there are no grapes on the vines;
> even though the olive crop fails,
> and the fields lie empty and barren;

> even though the flocks die in the fields,
> and the cattle barns are empty.
> —Habakkuk 3:17

Anyone looking out on that scene would feel pretty depressed, because those circumstances seem pretty hopeless. However, Habakkuk gives us a powerful "even if" lesson on how we can choose to live when heartache and hardship come our way. He said:

> yet I will rejoice in the Lord!
> I will be joyful in the God of my salvation!
> The Sovereign Lord is my strength!
> He makes me as surefooted as a deer,
> able to tread upon the heights.
> —Habakkuk 3:18-19

That word *yet* is about a choice that he was willing to make. Habakkuk chose to find his joy in God rather than melt down into the circumstances around him. Not only that, but the prophet knew that God would give him the strength to thrive in his faith, not just struggle from one day to the next.

Amen.

We've come a long way, haven't we? Not only have we learned what it means to fight in faith and win against worry, but we've learned so much about the Book of Joshua. However, the story of the Israelites' settling into the Promised Land doesn't end with the final chapter of the Book of Joshua. Keep reading through the Old Testament historical books, such as Judges, to discover whether all twelve tribes eventually claim their victory.

Even after you close the pages of this book never forget that experiencing victory and holding onto victory come from the same recipe: fighting in faith. Never let a worry discourage you. Instead, always see a worry as an opportunity to fight in faith and experience God's sweet victory! God's made many promises of peace, courage, and strength to you. He's promised to give you victory in every place of worry in your life.

If there are times when you falter in your worry battle, ask God for help. He won't turn you away! Never let Satan shame you out of your past, present, or future victories! You belong to God, and Romans 8:1 reminds us that God's children are never condemned because Jesus's sacrifice freed them from condemnation. If you are struggling today, you are free to run to God right now!

At the end of Joshua, he makes a covenant with them, committing them to follow God's ways. As followers of Jesus, we live under the New Covenant. Because of Jesus's sacrificial death on the cross, we are forgiven when we sin against God. Unlike the Old Covenant of rules, the currency of the New Covenant is God's grace and our faith. This Covenant is sealed by our faith in Christ and His finished work on the cross, and it is eternal. We might say that it's a "Big C" Covenant that covers every area of our lives. But we also can make "little c" covenants with God—agreements about specific areas of our lives that we are committing to work on with the help of the Holy Spirit.

Would you consider entering into a "little c" covenant agreement with God regarding your worry battle? A covenant agreement related to worry isn't a sacred document, and it does not replace your personal relationship with Jesus Christ. It's simply an agreement that confirms your decision to continue taking steps in your battle against worry in a way that glorifies God and positions you for victory.

My friend, God has promised to give you peace, courage, and strength through the Holy Spirit who lives within you. He has promised to give you victory in every area of worry in your life. My prayer for you is that this agreement will help align your heart's desire with your actions—both now and in the future.

Are you ready?

Covenant Agreement

- I agree that I will immediately battle any worry that surfaces in my life and not allow weariness, compromise, apathy, or doubt to cause me to give up the battle.
- I agree that my fighting friends, *peace, courage,* and *strength,* are gifts from God for me to train and develop in order to fight in faith and receive God's power over worry.
- I agree that I have been resourced with fighting tools and resources so that I will never be without help to battle worry.
- I agree that my worry battle is for me to fight, but only God can provide the victory.
- I agree that there is never a worry battle too big that God cannot win for me.
- I agree that if I worry, panic, or have a meltdown, as soon as I am able, I will acknowledge my struggle and call out to God for help.
- I agree that I will not condemn myself for worry, but I will not compromise for anything less than victory.
- I agree that God will receive the glory for any victories, and I will gladly share my story to encourage others toward God for help.

Signed: _____

Date: _____

Afterword

riend, our time together has come to an end. But I want to leave you with one final encouragement. As you know, Christians often say the word *amen*. Do you know what *amen* actually means? It means "let it be true."[1]

As I think about everything that we've read, answered, learned, and experienced, my deepest prayer is that your desire is to not lose any ground that you've gained in your battle against worry. I hope that as various lessons resonate in your heart, you will want to hold on to those lessons and keep them close by always.

So, as we share one final prayer, I want you to emphasize the "amen" at the end to affirm your final desire to continue the road that you've traveled. It has been a joy sharing this journey with you. It's now my privilege to offer this final prayer for you.

> God, thank You for walking with my friend through this experience. Whatever changes she's seen in her life and whatever victories she's experienced, I praise You for them. I pray that in the days ahead she will continue to fight in faith for the glory of Your name.
>
> Remind her of Joshua's faithfulness when she hears those worry whispers.
>
> Remind her of Your promises to fight for her when circumstances feel like giant worry walls that block her way.

Remind her of Your promise to give her peace when she feels panic, and pick her up after a meltdown with the whisper from Your word or the encouragement of a friend.

Most of all, God, never let her forget that victory over worry is hers as long as she's fighting with You.

Thank You, God for giving us the power to live worry-free! While we may not be 100 percent there yet, we know that You will give us victory as we trust in You.

Now, my friend, this is where you say along with me...
Amen.

Notes

1. What Kind of Worrier Are You?

1. Dictionary.com, s.v. "worry," accessed October 29, 2017, www.dictionary.com/browse/worry.

2. Therese J. Borchard, "The Differences Between Normal Worry and General Anxiety Disorder," PsychCentral, updated September 25, 2014, https://psychcentral.com/blog/archives/2014/01/02/the-differences-between-normal-worry-general-anxiety-disorder/.

3. ADAA, "Facts & Statistics," Anxiety and Depression Association of America, accessed November 30, 2017, https://adaa.org/about-adaa/press-room/facts-statistics.

4. T. J. Meyer, M. L. Miller, R. L. Metzger, T. D. Borkovec, "Development and Validation of the Penn State Worry Questionnaire," *Behaviour Research and Therapy* 28 (1990): 487–95. See https://outcometracker.org/library/PSWQ.pdf.

5. *Friends*, season 6, episode 9, "The One Where Ross Got High," directed by Kevin Bright, written by Greg Malins, aired November 25, 1999, on NBC.

6. Alex Gray, "What Are People in Your Country Most Worried About?" World Economic Forum, February 21, 2017, www.weforum.org/agenda/2017/02/what-are-people-in-your-country-most-worried-about.

2. Cliffhangers

1. "Heisenberg Uncertainty Principle," Chegg Study, accessed November 30, 2017, www.chegg.com/homework-help/definitions/heisenberg-uncertainty-principle-2.

2. Michael Komara, *Life in the Balance: 7 Strategies for Making Life Work* (Elk Lake, MI: Elk Lake Publishing, 2013), 12.

3. Gilda Radner, *It's Always Something*, 20th anniv. ed. (New York: Simon & Schuster, 2015), 254.

4. Archy O. de Berker et al., "Computations of Uncertainty Mediate Acute Stress Responses in Humans," *Nature Communications* 7 (2016): 10996, www.nature.com/articles/ncomms10996.

5. Wayne Grudem, *Systematic Theology: An Introduction to Biblical Doctrine* (Grand Rapids, MI: Zondervan, 1994), 119.

3. Eight-Legged Worry

1. David Rock, "Why Do So Many Self-Help Books Sound the Same?" *Psychology Today*, August 30, 2009, www.psychologytoday.com/blog /your-brain-work/200908/why-do-so-many-self-help-books-sound -the-same.

4. How Do You Stop a Worry?

1. Nick Chordas, "2 Ohioans at Center of Story of Heroism," *Columbus Dispatch*, November 9, 2010, www.dispatch.com/content/stories/life _and_entertainment/2010/11/09/2-ohioans-at-center-of-story-of -heroism.html.

2. "THE Longest and Heaviest Train OFFICIALLY in the World," footage of the Australian BHP ore train, February 24, 2008, www .youtube.com/watch?v=9LsuNWjRaAo.

3. Simon A. Rego and Jennifer L. Taitz, "Worry Less Report: A White Paper on the Prevalence of Worrying & Coping Mechanisms for Americans at Home or on the Road," Liberty Mutual Insurance, accessed December 1, 2017, www.libertymutualgroup.com/about-liberty-mutual -site/news-site/Documents/LMI%20Worry%20Less%20White%20 Paper%20FINAL.pdf, p. 3.

4. Caroline Leaf, *Switch on Your Brain: The Key to Peak Happiness, Thinking and Health* (Grand Rapids, MI: Baker, 2013), 33, 46.

5. Russ Rankin, "Study: Bible Engagement in Churchgoers' Hearts,

Not Always Practiced," LifeWay, accessed December 1, 2017, www
.lifeway.com/Article/research-survey-bible-engagement-churchgoers.

6. Peter Dizikes, "When the Butterfly Effect Took Flight," *MIT Technology Review*, February 22, 2011, www.technologyreview.com/s /422809/when-the-butterfly-effect-took-flight/.

7. Chuck Swindoll, *Growing Strong in the Seasons of Life* (Grand Rapids: Zondervan, 1994), 61.

5. Your Three Fighting Friends

1. G. K. Chesterton, *Chesterton Day by Day: The Wit and Wisdom of G. K. Chesterton*, ed. Michael W. Perry (Seattle: Inkling, 2002), January 3.

2. J. Maxwell Miller and Gene M. Tucker, *The Book of Joshua: The Cambridge Bible Commentary on the New English Bible*, Cambridge Bible Commentaries (Cambridge, UK: Cambridge University Press, 1974, 2008), 36–37.

6. The Cure for "Fast Forgetting"

1. Patricia Sullivan, "Terry Ryan, 60; Wrote the Memoir 'The Prize Winner of Defiance, Ohio,'" *Washington Post*, May 18, 2007, www .washingtonpost.com/wp-dyn/content/article/2007/05/18/AR2007 051802025.html.

2. Caroline Leaf, *Switch on Your Brain: The Key to Peak Happiness, Thinking and Health* (Grand Rapids, MI: Baker, 2013), 63.

3. Bangambiki Habyarimana, *Inspirational Quotes for All Occasions* (Lulu.com, n.d.), chap. 64.

4. Braelee Stewart, in conversation with the author, June 25, 2017.

5. Anne Voskamp, "When You're feeling a Bit Broken," Anne Voskamp blog, April 4, 2011, http://annvoskamp.com/2011/04/when-youre -feeling-a-bit-broken-free-weekly-gratitude-journal/.

7. When You Can't See Around Your Situation

1. Ronald F. Youngblood, *Nelson's New Illustrated Bible Dictionary* (Nashville: Thomas Nelson, 2000), 647.

2. Bryant Wood, "The Walls of Jericho," Answers in Genesis, March 1,

1999, https://answersingenesis.org/archaeology/the-walls-of-jericho/.

3. Leander E. Keck et al., ed., *Introduction to Narrative Literature, Joshua, Judges, Ruth, 1 & 2 Samuel, 1 & 2 Kings, 1 & 2 Chronicles*, vol. 2 of *The New Interpreter's Bible Commentary* (Nashville: Abingdon Press, 2015), 47.

4. L. A. Artis, *Dark Blessing: The Power, Joy, and Blessings That Are Released Because of the Dark Times in Your Life* (n.p.: Xulon, 2007), 222.

8. Circumcision of the Heart

1. C. S. Lewis, *Letter to Malcolm: Chiefly on Prayer* (1964; New York: HarperOne, 2017), 56.

9. God, If...

1. Rob Blackhurst, "Mass Appeal: The Secret to Rick Warren's Success," *Financial Times*, reprinted on *Slate*, August 14, 2011, www.slate.com/articles/life/ft/2011/08/mass_appeal.html.

2. J. Hampton Keathley III, "The Captain of the Lord's Army (Joshua 5:13-15)," Bible.org, accessed December 5, 2017, https://bible.org/article/captain-lord's-army-joshua-513-15.

3. "Fly Away," track 8 on Lenny Kravitz, 5, Virgin Records, 1998.

10. God, Knock Down My Worry Walls

1. Phil Vischer, "Keep Walking," from *Josh and the Big Wall!* Everland Entertainment, 2002, VHS.

2. Richard Foster, *Celebration of the Disciplines* (New York: HarperCollins, 1998).

11. In Case of a Meltdown...

1. Harvard Health Publishing, "Anxiety and Physical Illness," Harvard.edu, July 2008, updated June 6, 2017, www.health.harvard.edu/staying-healthy/anxiety_and_physical_illness.

2. Commentary on Joshua 7:6 at BibleHub.com, accessed December 5, 2017, http://biblehub.com/commentaries/joshua/7-6.htm.

3. Martin Seligman, *Learned Optimism: How to Change Your Mind and Your Life* (New York: A. A. Knopf, 1991).

12. What if God Doesn't Give Me What I Want?

1. Dennis T. Lane, ed., *The Holy Bible English Standard Version: the ESV Study Bible* (Wheaton, IL: Crossway, 2009), 405.

2. "7200. Raah," BibleHub, accessed December 5, 2017, http://bible hub.com/hebrew/7200.htm.

3. *Ellicott's Commentary for English Readers*, commentary on Exodus 20:17, BibleHub, accessed December 5, 2017, http://biblehub.com /commentaries/ellicott/exodus/20.htm.

4. *Ellicott's Commentary*.

5. David Kalas, *When Did God Become a Christian?* (Nashville: Abingdon Press, 2017), 104, quoting Theodoret of Cyr, *Ancient Christian Commentary of Scripture, Old Testament XIV* (Downer's Grove, IL: InterVarsity, 2003), 2.

6. Melissa Spoelstra, *Numbers: Learning Contentment in a Culture of More* (Nashville: Abingdon Press, 2017), 146.

7. Tam Hodge, *And Now I Choose: A Story for Those Who Believe They Have No Choice* (n.p.: CreateSpace, 2014), 81.

8. Hodge, *And Now I Choose*, 85, 83.

9. Hodge, *And Now I Choose*, 84.

10. Hodge, *And Now I Choose*, 87.

13. Are You a Worrier or a Warrior?

1. Emily J. Teipe, "Will the Real Molly Pitcher Please Stand Up?" *National Archives* 31, no. 2 (summer 1999), www.archives.gov /publications/prologue/1999/summer/pitcher.html.

2. Lisa Bevere, *Girls with Swords: How to Carry Your Cross Like a Hero* (Colorado Springs: Waterbrook, 2014).

3. Harold Stephens, quoted in Linda Mintle, *Letting Go of Worry* (Eugene, OR: Harvest House, 2011), 17.

15. Does Your Hurry Cause Worry?

1. Megan Garber, "The Clocks at Grand Central Station Are Permanently Wrong," *Atlantic*, February 1, 2013, www.theatlantic.com /technology/archive/2013/02/the-clocks-at-grand-central-station-are -permanently-wrong/272768/.

2. Lucy Swindoll, quoted in Christa Kinde, *Finding Freedom from Worry and Stress* (Nashville: Thomas Nelson, 2003), 24.

3. Anne Fisher, "Too Busy to Think? You May Suffer from 'Hurry Sickness,'" *Fortune*, February 4, 2015, http://fortune.com/2015/02/04 /busy-hurry-work-stress/.

4. Ann Voskamp. *The Broken Way (with Bonus Content): A Daring Path into the Abundant Life* (Grand Rapids: Zondervan, 2016), 59.

5. Voskamp, *The Broken Way*, 63.

6. Lauren Gaskill, phone conversation with author, November 8, 2017.

7. Steven Furtick, *Sun Stand Still* (Colorado Springs: Multnomah, 2010), 6.

8. Furtick, *Sun Stand Still*, 8.

9. Priscilla Shirer, *God Is Able* (Nashville: B&H, 2013), 94.

10. Don Stewart, "Did the Sun Actually Stand Still in Joshua's Long Day?" Blue Letter Bible FAQ page, accessed December 5, 2017, www .blueletterbible.org/faq/don_stewart/don_stewart_625.cfm.

11. John Ortberg, *Soulkeeping: Caring for the Most Important Part of You* (Grand Rapids, MI: Zondervan, 2014), 20.

16. How to Slay All Day

1. Tony Schwartz and Catherine McCarthy, "Manage Your Energy, Not Your Time," *Harvard Business Review*, October 2007, https://hbr .org/2007/10/manage-your-energy-not-your-time.

17. Secret Weapon

1. Oxford Living Dictionaries, s.v. "fast," accessed December 6, 2017, https://en.oxforddictionaries.com/definition/fast.

2. "3341. metanoia," BibleHub, accessed December 6, 2017, http://biblehub.com/greek/3341.htm.

3. David Guzik, "The Temptation of Jesus and His First Galilean Ministry," Study Guide for Matthew 4, Blue Letter Bible, accessed December 6, 2017, www.blueletterbible.org/Comm/archives/guzik_david/studyguide_mat/mat_4.cfm.

4. Abraham Lincoln, "Proclamation 97—Appointing a Day of National Humiliation, Fasting, and Prayer," March 30, 1863, The American Presidency Project, www.presidency.ucsb.edu/ws/?pid=69891.

5. Richard Foster, *Celebration of the Disciplines* (New York: HarperCollins, 1998), 55.

6. David Mathis, "Fasting for Beginners," Desiring God, August 26, 2015, www.desiringgod.org/articles/fasting-for-beginners.

7. Joe DeCena, keynote address, CEO Spartan Races, EPIC Leadership Summit, Toledo, Ohio, November 9, 2017.

8. Bill Bright, "How to Begin Your Fast," www.cru.org/us/en/train-and-grow/spiritual-growth/fasting/7-steps-to-fasting.2.html, accessed December 12, 2017.

18. Four Ways to Ruin a Good Fight

1. See Erin Fotherg et al., "Persistent Metabolic Adaptation 6 Years after 'The Biggest Loser' Competition," *Obesity* 24, no. 8 (August 2016): 1612–19, http://onlinelibrary.wiley.com/doi/10.1002/oby.21538/full.

2. Julie Mazziotta, "*Biggest Loser* Contestants to Speak Out on Gaining Back the Weight," *People*, May 2, 2016, http://people.com/bodies/the-biggest-loser-contestants-permanently-harm-their-metabolism-says-study/.

3. If you struggle with why God allowed so much destruction and murder in Canaan, check out my *Joshua: Winning the Worry Battle* six-week Bible study. In it we tackle those tough questions, and you search the Scriptures for yourself—not just to find answers but also to learn more about God and how He loves you, hates sin, and sacrificed greatly to give us victory over everything in life and eternity that threatens to hurt us.

4. David Guzik, "The Remaining Land; Allotments East of the Jordan," Study Guide for Joshua 13, Blue Letter Bible, www.blueletterbible.org /Comm/guzik_david/StudyGuide2017-Jos/Jos-13.cfm?a=200006.

5. "3528. Nikaó," BibleHub, accessed December 6, 2017, http://bible hub.com/greek/3528.htm.

19. Asking for God's Best

1. Lynn Cowell, *Make Your Move with DVD: Finding Unshakable Confidence Despite Your Fears and Failures* (Nashville: Thomas Nelson, 2017), 52.

2. John Piper, "Children, Heirs, and Fellow Sufferers," Desiring God, April 21, 2002, www.desiringgod.org/messages/children-heirs-and -fellow-sufferers.

20. Carefrontations

1. Jeff Nelson, "*American Idol*'s Mandisa Was Suicidal, Gained 200 Lbs. After Friend's Death: 'I'm Still Here' After Feeling 'So Hopeless.'" *People*, May 19, 2017, http://people.com/music/mandisa-suicidal-depression -weight-gain-after-friends-death/.

2. Trisha Yearwood, "Trisha Yearwood's Life-Changing Moments," *Good Housekeeping*, April 7, 2010, www.goodhousekeeping.com/life /inspirational-stories/interviews/a18821/trisha-yearwood-life -changing-moments/.

Afterword

1. *Strong's Concordance*, s.v. "amen," accessed December 11, 2017, http://biblehub.com/hebrew/5707.htm.

Made in the USA
Coppell, TX
21 April 2022

76872040R00134